echoes
of HIS
PRESENCE

echoes
of HIS
PRESENCE

STORIES OF THE
MESSIAH
FROM THE PEOPLE
OF HIS DAY

RAY VANDER LAAN
WITH JUDITH MARKHAM

ZondervanPublishingHouse
Grand Rapids, Michigan

A Division of HarperCollinsPublishers

Echoes of His Presence
Copyright © 1996 by Ray Vander Laan
First Zondervan edition 1998.

Requests for information should be addressed to:

ZondervanPublishingHouse
Grand Rapids, Michigan 49530

Library of Congress Cataloging-in-Publication Data

Vander Laan, Ray.
    Echoes of His presence: stories of the Messiah from the people of His day / Ray Vander
Laan with Judith Markham.
        p.   cm.
    Originally published: Colorado Springs : Focus on the Family, c 1996.
    Includes bibliographical references.
    ISBN: 0-310-67886-2
    1. Jesus Christ—Biography.   I. Markham, Judith E.   II Title.
BT301.2.V315   1998
232.9—dc21

                                    98-28284
                                        CIP

This edition printed on acid-free paper and meets the American National Standards Institute
Z39.48 standard.

Printed in the United States of America

    01 02 03 04 05 /❖ DC/ 10 9 8 7 6 5 4

To my wonderful wife, Esther

Her complete devotion to her family, to me, and most of all, to her God and His purpose have been an inspiring example to everyone who knows her. Her constant enthusiasm and encouragement throughout our life together have given me a fuller understanding of why a wife of noble character is worth far more than rubies (Proverbs 31:10).

Contents

Preface
Introduction: Jesus of Nazareth

Part 1: Who He Was

1. The Promise 1
2. The Bridegroom 11
3. The Good Shepherd 21
4. The King 31

Part 2: How He Taught

5. The Rabbi 45
6. The Prayer Shawl 61
7. The Theater 77
8. The Zealot 87
9. The Decapolis 97
10. The Living Water 109

Part 3: What He Did

11. The Jericho Road 127
12. The Triumphal Entry 139
13. The Gethsemane 149
14. The Final Sacrifice 161
15. The Feast of Pentecost 171

Glossary 189
Annotated Bibliography 191
Maps: First-Century Israel 193
        First-Century Galilee 195

Preface

My life has been a spiritual journey. From childhood, I was taught about God and His love and instilled with a respect for His Word. I knew that Jesus was sent as God's Messiah and that He was born among the Jewish people in the first century. But the journey of my faith has taken me from an intellectual understanding that Jesus was Jewish to an experiential awareness of how significant it is to understand and hear Jesus in His role as a rabbi, speaking, teaching, and acting in ways that were normal to the Jews of His day.

Nearly every year for the past 20 years, I've spent several weeks in Israel. Walking the land itself and getting to know the people has not only enabled me to envision what it must have been like for the people who heard Jesus, or heard of Him, but has also made His message and presence in my own life clearer. This book is a result of that journey and an attempt to encourage others to think about who Jesus was in the context in which God placed Him.

To that end, God used several significant influences in my life to prompt me to begin the journey and to create within me a passion for seeking to understand what it means that God sent His Son into a Jewish world. Early in my ministry, I was introduced to the writings of the late Abraham Heschel, who so clearly explored the relationship between Judaism and Christianity and stimulated a curiosity in me that has never faded. And while I was at the American Institute of Holy Land Studies in Jerusalem, Jim Monson, lecturer and teacher, inspired within me a love and passion for the land of Israel and the Jewish people.

God has also provided many individuals who have encouraged me and shaped my thinking. Among them is Donald P. Wisse, my senior pastor for many years. He always encouraged me to pursue the emphasis that I felt so strongly and to share it in the life of the congregation. His enthusiasm for the Word of God, and his desire for his congregation to grow in their understanding of that Word, helped me to appreciate what God wants from those whom He has called to be shepherds of His people. In both subtle and direct ways, the Jewish scholars and rabbis I encountered during my days in New Jersey encouraged me to recognize the Jewish roots of my own faith. And, finally, I'm greatly indebted to my very good friends David and Hannah Binstein, in Israel. They have always encouraged me to understand how the culture of the people of the Bible fits the land of Israel so perfectly, a land they've been a part of their whole lives and love with a passion that only Israelis understand.

In the writing of this book, there have been several individuals whose support and encouragement have been significant.

Judith Markham has not only been a most encouraging and helpful writer and editor, but she has also become a good friend whose passion for understanding the land and the people of Israel matches my own. Without her efforts, this book could never have happened.

I want to thank the Focus on the Family organization for its desire to publish this material and for its encouragement and strengthening of families and individual Christians through its ministry. In particular, I appreciate the support of Dr. James Dobson. I will always value the time we spent together in Israel seeking to understand Jesus and the mission He gave to the people of God. In the Publishing Department, Michele Kendall, an outstanding editor and patient critic, and Al Janssen, an enthusiastic supporter, made this work possible.

I would also like to thank the board of Holland Christian High School; Stan Koster, my superintendent; and Dr. Tim Hoeksema, my principal, for granting me the sabbatical to do the Israel project, including this book. Their vision for the larger world of Christian education outside of Holland, Michigan, has been an example and encouragement to me.

Most of all, I'd like to express my gratitude to God for my family. This book and the other projects that went with it have taken me away from my family for significant amounts of time and have distracted me from them and important times in their lives. They have made great sacrifices so that this work could be accomplished.

To my father and mother: You taught me to love the Lord before I was old enough to understand what that meant. Your desire to be faithful to Him, to be His witnesses in everything you did, has shaped my life in profound ways.

To Jeff, Charity, Michelle, Lisa, and Alison: I love you more than you'll ever know, and my increasing understanding of the significance of family in the Jewish context has caused me to rededicate my desire to be the godly father all of you deserve.

To my wife, Esther: You were convinced this book was part of God's purpose, and you never wavered in your commitment to its completion. Your support, encouragement, and enthusiasm have made it possible.

Echoes of His Presence is neither a systematic treatment of the Judaism of Jesus' time nor an academic treatise. I'm a teacher and pastor, using the gifts God gave me to share what I've learned through my studies.

My hope and prayer is that this book will be used by God to help readers see and appreciate the reality of the person and work of Jesus and to spark an interest and desire in them to pursue a deeper understanding of the Jewish roots of the faith God has given us through our Jewish Messiah and His faithful disciples.

R.V.L.
February 1996

Introduction
Jesus of Nazareth

From the beginning, God spoke and acted within the context of human culture. It was not unusual, then, that His Son should do the same.

Jesus lived like a Jew, talked like a Jew, acted like a Jew, and worshiped like a Jew. He *was* a Jew—a Jew from Nazareth. Thus, His words, actions, and teaching methods were in keeping with the customs, traditions, and religion of the Semitic culture into which He was born.

If we are to more fully understand and appreciate Jesus and His teachings, we need to recognize this. When we do, we fall in love with Him all over again.

To gain a clearer picture, however, we must leave our twentieth-century culture and our Western attitudes and travel back to the first-century world Jesus inhabited. We need to journey to another time and place . . . to the land of Israel, to the birthplace and home of Jesus. We must step into a culture that was Eastern and extremely religious, a culture in which families played an important role.

All these factors figure into any understanding of people's reactions to Jesus and His ministry.

Who He Was

Jesus Christ, the Son of God incarnate, the Word made flesh, entered our human world at a specific time and place.

He wasn't born in northwestern Iowa, in Southern California, in the Texas panhandle, or in the Appalachian Mountains. He was born in a land that was a hotbed of political and religious turmoil, a country that had been the crossroads of the world for centuries, where the rocky soil was red with the blood of the conquered and the conquerors. He was born into a race of people chosen by God to bear His name to the world; a people who had made a covenant with God and broken it—and then been restored to His favor. They were a passionate people, religiously and politically, but they had not been completely free for more than 500 years.

Though He lived a perfect life and provided the final, perfect sacrifice for sin, Jesus was not some extraterrestrial being who floated on clouds in a halo of blond curls. Jesus was a rabbi; He was a stonemason and carpenter. He knew

wed a particular rabbi "took his yoke": They
d's Word.
stry, therefore, His methods were easily recog-
downers, Pharisees, and ordinary people called
Rabbi."

/as a member of His culture. Though His message
the people—Jews and Gentiles—using methods
His role as a first-century Jewish rabbi who was
rolled country.
s life and actions. Though He lived a pure life,
ich no other man had ever done or ever could do,
a fulfillment of God's promise centuries before to
s' ministry was carried out according to the struc-
th His people Israel.
aid the price for the breaking of the covenant God
e came as a sacrificial lamb, completing, once and
nstructed Moses to establish. His redemptive work
ast system God had given to the Israelites and that
ish people of Jesus' day.
into Jerusalem on the day the sacrificial lamb was
was also sacrificed on the cross during Passover, the
ts. He was buried at the beginning of the Feast of
that, among other things, offered thanks to God for
vided from the earth. Jesus was then buried so that
e earth. And He rose on the Feast of Firstfruits, the
inning of the harvest.

ndeed been raised from the dead, the firstfruits
fallen asleep. For since death came through a
on of the dead comes also through a man. For
so in Christ all will be made alive. But each in
ist, the firstfruits; then, when he comes, those
(1 Corinthians 15:20–23)

Holy Spirit on Shavuot, or Pentecost, the second of the

ew, you can begin to see how understanding Jesus'

culture enriches not only our insight into His redemptive actions but also gives us a more *dynamic* picture of his life and work.

As You Read

Each of the following chapters contains three main elements: a selection of Scripture passages that point directly to the area of Christ's life or ministry under discussion; a story highlighting events and circumstances of the culture at that time; and an explanation of how elements revealed in the story apply directly to *our* lives today.

While the characters in the following stories are imaginary, most of the details—the land, the places, the political situations, the historical events—are not. The descriptions of the customs, religious beliefs, and everyday practices are based on a growing body of research.

In many instances, I've used the Hebrew/Aramaic names and terms, rather than their English renderings—for example, Yochanan for John or Jonathan, Shmu'el for Samuel, Moshe for Moses, and Yerushalayim for Jerusalem. These words are footnoted and defined the first time they appear in the text. For easy reference, all are included in a glossary at the back of the book.

I've also incorporated a number of Hebrew terms that expand the meaning of our English translation of Scripture—for example, *tekton*, which means "builder," usually referring to a stonemason but often translated as "carpenter"; and *tzitzit*, which means "tassel," as on a Jewish prayer shawl. I have used these terms interchangeably with the English words or meanings and have footnoted the first usage and included them in the glossary.

Since many of the original Hebrew/Aramaic words had several shades or nuances of meaning (as do our English words), I've tried to indicate that when it is relevant or important. For example, "rabbi," "teacher," and "master" are interchangeable, but taken together, they show the various levels and richness of that relationship and calling.

Since the Jews never said the name of God, in dialogue passages I've often used synonyms for God, such as Adonai or the Almighty.

Through these characters and their stories, I want you to see the beauty of the silvery green olive trees on the Galilean hillsides. I want you to feel the rocks beneath your feet and the burning sun on your back. I want you to smell the dust and feel your mouth dry up with thirst. I want you to climb the heights of the awesome Judean Mountains and wander the lonely expanse of the wilderness. I want you to smell the spices and the fresh bread baking in the market-

catch fish, and live in the shadow of the kings and wore tassels on the hem of His tunic, attended in the everyday household of a Galilean insula es' seat in the synagogue. He stubbed His toes on dusty and dirty, and He perspired and got thirsty in Wilderness.

n't diminish our Savior. It only makes the fact that ce it for us more astounding and overwhelming.

so called masters and teachers—frequently traveled g in towns, villages, and local synagogues wherever hese religious teachers had a trade and could earn a epended on the generosity of others for their daily ted to attend banquets and weddings and to stay in eadily shared meals with both old friends and new

out Judea and Galilee, rabbis visited both local syna- n Jerusalem with their talmidim—the disciples or m. "To make many talmidim" is a Jewish expression refers to the rabbis' practice of collecting disciples. r example, Gamaliel, the apostle Paul's teacher, had

n a student of religion, however. While he certainly study of his rabbi's interpretations of the Law (also ve books of Moses) and the Prophets, a talmid was, by t to become like his master.

ching methods to interpret the Torah. One of the most f parables. Today, over 3,000 parables still survive from

creative use of their surroundings. Whether indoors or ete things, such as flowers, trees, birds, fish, water, and ical concepts.

tradition, phrases such as "You've heard it said . . . but r it is written . . ." were common.

us interpretations of the Torah, a talmid was committed t by his own rabbi. This was called "taking the yoke of place. I want you to hear the babble of voices from many lands as you press through the congested maze of Jerusalem's narrow streets.

Above all, I hope that through these pages you will gain a fresh perspective on the message and ministry of our Savior and become increasingly aware of the echoes of His presence in your own life.

Part 1

Who He Was

Chapter 1

The Promise

Abram believed the LORD, and he credited it to him as right-eousness.

He also said to him, "I am the LORD, who brought you out of Ur of the Chaldeans to give you this land to take possession of it."

But Abram said, "O Sovereign LORD, how can I know that I will gain possession of it?"

So the LORD said to him, "Bring me a heifer, a goat and a ram, each three years old, along with a dove and a young pigeon."

Abram brought all these to him, cut them in two and arranged the halves opposite each other; the birds, however, he did not cut in half. . . . When the sun had set and darkness had fallen, a smoking firepot with a blazing torch appeared and passed between the pieces. On that day the LORD made a covenant with Abram and said, "To your descendants I give this land."

(Genesis 15:6–10,17–18)

When Abram was ninety-nine years old, the LORD appeared to him and said, "I am God Almighty; walk before me and be blame-less. I will confirm my covenant between me and you and will greatly increase your numbers." . . .

1

Then God said to Abraham, "As for you, you must keep my covenant, you and your descendants after you for the generations to come. This is my covenant with you and your descendants after you, the covenant you are to keep."

(Genesis 17:1–2,9–10)

The Northern Negev, A.D. 27

orty years in this desert wilderness. What must that have been like? Yochanan[1] wondered.

He and his rabbi had been traveling for only three weeks, yet it was beginning to feel like forever. The two of them had left their hometown of Capernaum, trekked down the Jordan Valley to Yericho,[2] and then climbed through the steep mountain passes to Yerushalayim.[3] The city of Daveed,[4] golden in the morning light. After visiting the Temple, they had headed south through the foothills of the Judean Mountains. Now they were nearing the place where Jahweh had made His presence known to their people.

"Forty years He forced them to wander here," Yochanan said. "After 400 years slaving for the Egyptians. What kind of God does that to His people?"

"A just and righteous one," replied the rabbi. "And a gracious one."

"How can you say that?" Yochanan said angrily—and a bit fearfully. After all, he was only 17, and this man was his teacher.

Hoping to become a rabbi one day, Yochanan had chosen to follow this respected teacher from the synagogue at Capernaum. As their religion required, Yochanan would live and study with this man for several years, learning as much as he could about the Torah[5] and the Haphtarah.[6] Someday he hoped to be both as wise and as righteous as his teacher.

"Listen, my son," said the rabbi. "You have heard it said that it was cruel of the Almighty to treat His chosen people in such a manner. But I tell you, those 40 years were not wasted."

"What do you mean?" Yochanan asked.

"Let's climb up there and I'll explain." The rabbi pointed toward a hill rising

---

1. John
2. Jericho
3. Jerusalem
4. David
5. The five books of Moses. The word *Torah* means "teachings," although it's often translated as "law."
6. The books of the Prophets

alone in the distance. The rolling countryside around it was brown from the heat of summer, although a recent shower had left traces of green on the plains. As they walked through the stony fields, Yochanan stripped off some ripe heads of wild wheat and munched on the sweet kernels.

When they reached the bottom of the hill, the teacher led the way, using the tumbled ruins of a wall as a stairway up the steep side. Halfway up, he stopped. Then, sweeping his arm from side to side, he indicated the landscape before them. Rolling hills and fields faded into the horizon as far as they could see. Sheep, goats, and camels ranged the countryside. Nomad tents and encampments dotted the plains.

"When this land and its people were already very old," said the teacher, "Moshe[7] led our people out of the wilderness in which they had wandered because of their disobedience. They had tried to enter the land once before, but the spies sent to scout out the territory were terrified by the sophisticated and fortified cities and the powerful inhabitants. The Philistines had iron; they had weapons our people had never seen before. Their city walls and fortresses were formidable. Our forefathers were shepherds and farmers, not soldiers."

"But Adonai[8] had promised them this land."

"Ah, yes. But to get it, they had to defeat the people who already lived here. And could they trust Adonai to fight the battle for them? That was the question. Ultimately, they did not trust the One who had led them safely all this way. Their disbelief sent them back for another 40-year trek in the wilderness south of here, camping from place to place—just like those nomads over there. One year for every day the spies were gone checking out the land." The teacher smiled as he added, "We are a people who have always needed concrete images. 'You'll learn to trust Me,' said the Almighty. And He meant it."

"What is this place?" Yochanan asked. "Why are we here?" They had come to an area where the crumbling remains of city walls crisscrossed the hillside.

"People have lived here for centuries. When one town was destroyed by earthquake or enemies, another was built on top of it. But be patient. We'll talk more about it when we get there," said the teacher, pointing to the summit. "Let's climb the rest of the way."

At the top of the hill a few minutes later, Yochanan saw the cobbled streets of an ancient city, wide enough for two to walk side by side. The building walls that formed the narrow passageways, though broken and cracked, still rose above their heads.

---

7. Moses
8. God

"What is this place?" the boy asked again as they walked along the uneven stones.

"This may have been the first city the desert wanderers came upon as they trekked north out of the wilderness," his teacher said. He went on to tell how this had been a Canaanite stronghold. Later, however, as God's people gradually occupied the land, this became a place of faith where the inhabitants built their own house of prayer by copying the Temple at Yerushalayim. Its walls of rough-cut stones had been fitted together, just like the Temple God had instructed King Solomon to build.

"Look," said the rabbi, leading Yochanan into a smaller, enclosed area. "Here we are in the place of worship. There is the holy place, the priests' court. And here is the altar."

The rabbi pointed to the remains of a seven-and-a-half-foot-high square of uncut stones with a stone ledge running along the front, halfway up. "The priest would have stood on that ledge when he made the sacrifices," said the rabbi. "At that place, every day at dawn and three—at the third and ninth hours of daylight—the priest offered the people's sacrifices and sprinkled the blood along the base of the altar."

Yochanan ran his hand over the sloped stone where the blood had been channeled from the altar. *At dawn and three every day this ran with blood,* he thought. *It must have been a bloody mess all the time.* Was that how God saw their sins? Bloody, messy, and stinking?

"Why did they keep doing it?" Yochanan asked. "Why do we? Do you ever wonder about that, Master? After all the sacrifices, what difference has it made?"

"We are part of a long line of people. We are part of a covenant made in blood by the Almighty. Therefore, we do it in remembrance. We are remembering Adonai's promise."

Then the rabbi pointed toward hills to the north. "Over there, just a few miles, is Hebron. That is where Avraham[9] was camped at the time the Almighty made the covenant with him," he said. "Avraham was still childless, though. How could Adonai keep His promise now? Avraham wondered. How could he become the father of a great nation when he didn't have even one son? Despite those misgivings, however, Avraham believed the One who had called him. And by doing that, he became the father of all who believe."

Yochanan noticed a smile cross his teacher's face.

"Still, our father Avraham wanted it spelled out. As I said, we Jews have always

9. Abraham

needed concrete images, even from the Almighty! So Avraham confronted the Almighty. 'How can I know for sure that all this will come to pass?' And Adonai said, 'Make Me a blood path, Avraham.'"

Yochanan shook his head in puzzlement. "A blood path? Of course I've heard of it, but I still don't understand."

"You'll see," was all his teacher would say. "We must be moving on now. We have a ways to go yet."

A few miles to the west, near the wells of Beersheba, they stopped for the night. As they made camp, Yochanan noticed bustling activity around the tents of one of the nearby nomad encampments. The spicy scent of smoke and roasting meat drifted their way, and the cooling night air carried excited voices and the stringed music of the kinnor.

"Come join us," one of the nomads called, beckoning.

"These desert dwellers are always hospitable," the rabbi said as the two walked toward the encampment. "They're eager to welcome strangers."

The nomad greeted them with a kiss. "We're celebrating the betrothal of my brother's oldest son. They're just about to seal the covenant."

Firelight reflected off the richly embroidered dresses adorning the women and young girls. Golden coins, fringing the edges of their veils, chimed musically as they moved. The men's festive headdresses, fastened around their foreheads with braided ropes, rippled softly in the evening breeze.

"Watch carefully," the rabbi murmured to Yochanan as the ceremony began.

At first the chatter and laughter increased as the gathered families clustered around an open area, away from the fire where the wives had been baking bread and brewing sweet tea. Then gradually the voices diminished, leaving only the shrill cries of the younger children.

Yochanan stood on tiptoe and stretched to see what was creating the drama in the air.

"That's the father of the bridegroom and the father of the bride," his teacher whispered as two men, each leading a goat, moved into the open space.

The animals struggled, fighting the guiding hands. The fire blazed higher as someone threw more sticks on it.

Each man drew a long knife from his sash. The people leaned closer. Knives gleamed silver, and red blood spurted.

The dying animals kicked, jerked, and were still.

Then the two fathers, robes splattered, held the severed throats of the animals

A Blood Covenant. One covenant-making ceremony called for each of the covenant makers to walk in animal blood to symbolize the life commitment of each party to the covenant. (*Charlie Shaw*)

so that the crimson liquid pooled onto the ground. The hot, sweet, metallic scent, both distasteful and compelling, filled Yochanan's nostrils.

The crowd stirred slightly again after the dramatic moment of slaughter. The two men laid the drained carcasses on either side of the darkening pool.

Then slowly, deliberately, each man took off his sandals and stepped barefoot into the pool of blood. The hems of their robes dripped red, and their bloody feet marked the path.

"Tonight this covenant has been sealed in blood," said the two men.

"May I pay with my life if this covenant is broken," each said to the other.

"You have just witnessed a covenant sealed with blood," said the teacher. He and Yochanan were walking back to their camp after sharing in the feast that had followed the ceremony. "Those two fathers have promised to keep that covenant at the cost of their own lives. Do you now understand the kind of covenant the Almighty made with our forefather Avraham?"

"Adonai walked through blood like that," Yochanan said. "For us." And again he asked, "What kind of God does such a thing?"

"The Father of Avraham, Yitzchak,[10] and Ya'akov,[11]" said the rabbi. "Your God."

Later, as they lay on the ground in their bedrolls, Yochanan looked up at the vast, dark sky filled with pinpricks of starlight. "All that blood," he said. "Surely the Almighty One would not have done that unless He meant it. But it's been so many years now. When is Adonai going to keep His promise? *How* is He going to keep His promise?"

"I don't know, my son," said the teacher. "Only the Almighty knows the time and place. Surely our ancestors broke their covenant with Him and deserved to pay the penalty. But remember, when He walked through that blood path for Avraham, Adonai promised, 'This is what will happen to Me, Avraham, if I do not keep My covenant with you. I will pay with My life if this covenant is broken.'"

> *Then Moses went up to God, and the LORD called to him from the mountain and said, "This is what you are to . . . tell the people of Israel: '. . . if you obey me fully and keep my covenant, then out of all nations you will be my treasured possession.'"*
>
> (Exodus 19:3–5)

What an awesome God we have! What incredible love He has for His creatures!

Imagine! The Creator of the universe, the holy and righteous God, was willing to leave heaven and come down to a nomad's tent in the dusty, hot desert of the Negev to express His love for His people.

"Bring me a heifer, a goat and a ram . . . along with a dove and a young pigeon," God told Abraham. Then, when those animals had been sacrificed and laid out on both sides of their shed blood, God made a covenant. To do that, He walked "barefoot," in the form of a blazing torch, through the path of blood between the animals.

Think of it. Almighty God walking barefoot through a pool of blood! The thought of a human being doing that is, to say the least, unpleasant. Yet God, in

---

10. Isaac
11. Jacob

all His power and majesty, expressed His love that personally. By participating in that traditional, Near Eastern covenant-making ceremony, He made it unavoidably clear to the people of that time, place, and culture what He intended to do.

"I love you so much, Abraham," God was saying, "and I promise that this covenant will come true for you and your children. I will never break My covenant with you. I'm willing to put My own life on the line to make you understand that."

Picturing God passing through that gory path between the carcasses of animals, imagining the blood splashing as He walked, helps us recognize the faithfulness of God's commitment. He was willing to express, in terms His chosen people could understand, that He would never fail to do what He promised. And He ultimately fulfilled His promise by giving His own life, His own blood, on the Cross.

Because we look at God's dealings with Abraham as some remote piece of history in a far-off land, we often fail to realize that we, too, are part of the long line of people with whom God made a covenant on that rocky plain near Hebron. And like those who came before us, we have broken that covenant.

When He walked in the dust of the desert and through the blood of the animals Abraham had slaughtered, God was making a promise to *all* the descendants of Abraham—to everyone in the household of faith. When God splashed through the blood, He did it for *us*.

We're not simply individuals in relationship to God. We're part of a long line of people marching back through history, from our famous Jewish ancestors David, Hezekiah, and Peter to the millions of unknown believers; from the ancient Israelites and the Jewish people of Jesus' day to the Christian community dating from the early church. We're part of a community of people with whom God established relationship in the dust and sand of the Negev.

But there's more. When God made covenant with His people, He did something no human being would have even considered doing. In the usual blood covenant, each party was responsible for keeping only his side of the promise. When God made covenant with Abraham, however, He promised to keep *both* sides of the agreement.

"If this covenant is broken, Abraham, for whatever reason—for My unfaithfulness or yours—I will pay the price," said God. "If you or your descendants, for whom you are making this covenant, fail to keep it, I will pay the price in blood."

And at that moment, Almighty God pronounced the death sentence on His Son Jesus.

Two thousand years later, on a hill outside Jerusalem, only 35 miles from the area where this covenant was made, Jesus, the Messiah, very God Himself in human form, hung on a cross, His blood dripping onto the same dusty, rocky soil upon which His ancestor and servant Abraham had walked.

God had kept His promise.

> *God presented him [Jesus] as a sacrifice of atonement, through faith in his blood.*
>
> (Romans 3:25a)

Chapter 2

The Bridegroom

As a young man marries a maiden, so will your sons marry you; as a bridegroom rejoices over his bride, so will your God rejoice over you.

(Isaiah 62:5)

In my Father's house are many rooms; if it were not so, I would have told you. I am going there to prepare a place for you. And if I go and prepare a place for you, I will come back and take you to be with me that you also may be where I am. You know the way to the place where I am going.

(John 14:2–4)

No one knows about that day or hour, not even the angels in heaven, nor the Son, but only the Father.

(Matthew 24:36)

The bride belongs to the bridegroom. The friend who attends the bridegroom waits and listens for him, and is full of joy when he hears the bridegroom's voice.

(John 3:29)

Korazin, A.D. 27

ikha'el's[1] heart pounded with exertion and excitement. Each stone he lifted and set in place brought him closer to the day he could bring Elisheva,[2] his bride, home.

As the youngest son, Mikha'el had watched his four brothers marry and bring their wives to his father's home. And before their weddings, each of his brothers had done what Mikha'el was now doing—adding his own living quarters to the many rooms that already surrounded the large courtyard.

Elisheva, he thought. *I'm glad I'm bringing her to this insula[3]—to this large, loving family. I wonder if she'll love them as much as I do?*

Mikha'el thought of the many hours he'd spent in the courtyard with his brothers and their wives, his sisters, his parents, his aunts and uncles, his cousins, his nephews and nieces. His family's insula complex was one of the largest in Korazin. Their family community now numbered more than 120 people.

When he stood on the flat roof of his father's house, he sometimes could hardly absorb all the beauty he saw. Rolling, green grasses carpeted the sloping valley that ended at the silver waters of Gennesaret.[4] Tall, stately cypress trees lined the road that wound around the sea, leading to the nearby village of Capernaum, nestled by the shore—where Elisheva lived.

Mikha'el brushed against the olive tree near the wall he was blocking up, and several of the silvery gray-green leaves spilled across his shoulder and onto the ground. One reason he had wanted to add his room at this end of the house was this tree. His father had told him many times that Israel was God's olive tree.

"God planted Israel, and when there was no fruit, He trimmed the tree back to the stump," his father said. "Now the shoots that sustain us grow from that

---

1. Michael
2. Elizabeth
3. (pl. insulae) A family household arrangement common in Capernaum and Korazin, where many rooms—residences for various family members—were built around a central courtyard.
4. Sea of Galilee; also known as the Sea of Tiberias after Herod Antipas's capital city, Tiberias, which he named for his friend the Roman emperor Tiberius.

Adding a Room. This reconstructed village of Qatzrin in Galilee dates to 200 years after Jesus. Yet the stone construction and the tools used had changed little from His time. The wooden scaffolding allowed the builders to place the stones in rows, with smaller stones to wedge them in place. (*Eyal Bartov*)

stump, our ancestors. And someday the Messiah will come from Yishai's[5] stump."

This tree will be a constant reminder of that, and its leaves rustling in the breeze will provide shade outside the window of my beloved, Mikha'el thought.

Just then he heard footsteps, and his grandmother hobbled around the nearest corner of the house, leaning stiffly on a stick of olive wood and clutching a small basket in her other hand. Though she was often troubled with the pains

---

5. Jesse

common to her age, each day she came out to check on his work and encourage him—and she always brought him something to eat. Today she offered him dried Yericho[6] figs.

"You're doing good work," she said as he eagerly popped a piece of the delicious fruit into his mouth. "You should be proud to bring your bride here."

"I am, Grandmother."

The elderly woman looked around at the grass, trampled by his coming and going. "You must ask your mother to help you plant some of her flowers here."

His mother had tamed the flowers of the field—bright-red poppies, golden mustard, and purple anemones—into a beautiful garden around their insula.

"I will," Mikha'el promised.

"Do it soon," his grandmother warned. "This is the season to plant them."

Yes, Mikha'el thought. *The seasons are passing.* When he had begun preparing a place for his bride, the spring sunshine had been bright and warm on his back. As he measured walls and framed stone archways for windows and doors, the gentle spring gave way to burning summer heat. Now the winter rainy season was fast approaching, and he was eager to be finished. Eager to see his betrothed and to start his own family.

"Don't be so impatient," his father kept telling him. "The care you take in preparing these rooms for your bride shows how much you love her."

Mikha'el knew his father was right. Yet waiting was hard. Fortunately, the work was hard also. When he wasn't busy at their family olive press, he was working on these rooms for his bride. Often he fell into bed at night so exhausted that he barely began sorting through his schemes and dreams before he drifted into sleep.

Before he slept, though, he always remembered to pray for Elisheva.

When a son or daughter came of marriageable age, every father wanted to arrange a good match for his child. As a good and dutiful son, Mikha'el would have accepted any bride his parents chose for him, but they had asked his preference.

"I would like to marry Elisheva," he'd said immediately.

He had known her since they were children. They had played together on the seashore, building rock fortresses and wading among the shallow reeds to catch tiny minnows in their hands. Elisheva had always been bright and funny, a good companion and childhood friend. And though Mikha'el had seen her only at a distance since she had come of marriageable age, he knew that she had grown

---

6. Jericho

into a fine young woman with a spotless reputation. Her God-fearing family went faithfully to the feasts at the Temple. In fact, their two families had often traveled to Yerushalayim[7] together.

When his father had told him it was time to begin thinking about a wife, Mikha'el's first thought was *Elisheva.* Because their fathers were lifelong friends, the marriage arrangements had not been difficult. The bride price Mikha'el's father had paid to Elisheva's father for the loss of his daughter had been a generous measure of olive oil.

Now, as he worked, Mikha'el's mind drifted back to the day of their engagement more than nine months ago. After the bride price had been paid, his father had poured a cup of wine from the flask he had carried to the ceremony.

As Mikha'el took the wine, he wondered fearfully, *When the cup is offered to Elisheva, will she take it? Will she dedicate her life to me? To our life together?*

Then he held the cup out to Elisheva and said, "By offering this cup, I vow that I am willing to give my life for you."

His skin flushed with warmth and his heart sang with joy when she held out her hand to take the cup from him.

After she drank, indicating that she was willing to give *her* life for him, he said to her, "I'm going to go back to Korazin and prepare a place for you, Elisheva. And when I'm finished, I'll come back and take you to be my wife." *And I'll work day and night so it won't be long,* he promised himself.

The joy of that moment warmed him now, even though the sun had disappeared behind the rain clouds gathering over Gennesaret. He could see several fishing boats clustered along the shore. Elisheva's father and brothers were fishermen. They might be in one of those boats, casting their nets across the water, hoping for a big catch.

Mikha'el walked across the field to gather more pieces of basalt. His brothers had helped him quarry a supply of the dark-gray rock from the hillside across the wadi, but the pile was dwindling now as his building neared completion. The stones were heavy, and he stopped to wipe his sweaty face with his sleeve. When he lifted his arm, the tassels of the prayer shawl under his tunic caught on a purple thistle. As he carefully loosened the prickers from the threads, he looked toward the path that wound through the hills to Capernaum.

Some night soon, he hoped. Some night soon, he and his friends would make their way down that path to the home of Elisheva's family. Though she didn't know the day or the hour when he would come, he hoped his bride would be

---

7. Jerusalem

prepared for him and that her unmarried attendants would be ready when she called them. He could almost hear their happy shouts, the music and laughter, and see the lamps and torches flickering in the darkness as the procession returned to this place he had built for her. Then, while the crowd gathered in the courtyard and Mikha'el's attendant stood outside the closed door of their room, he and Elisheva would consummate their marriage.

He hardly dared think about that long-anticipated moment. He knew Elisheva would be beautiful, with her dark, curly hair loose around her shoulders and her brown eyes sparkling with joy. At least he hoped she would be as happy as he was, as eager as he for their life together.

Father is right, he thought. *Making sure everything is prepared and perfect is important.* So many things to think about. Their rooms. His wedding garments. Flowers for Elisheva. *Oil!* He needed to make sure there was extra oil on hand from the family presses for the lamps of the wedding guests. It would not do to run out. And wine. Since the wedding feast would last for seven days, was there enough wine in the storeroom?

Was Elisheva as eager and flustered as he was? Even now she would be making her own preparations. Not just for the ceremony itself, but for their life together as well. At home with her mother, she would be learning to grind flour, bake, and cook. Elisheva's mother was a skillful weaver, both of cloth and baskets, and she would be teaching her daughter those skills and others—everything she needed to know to be a wife and mother herself. Elisheva would be doing all this to become the best bride she could be.

Though her bride price had been high, Mikha'el's father had paid it gladly, without hesitation. Now she belonged to Mikha'el, and he to her. No one else could claim her. Her life was his. Was she thinking the same of him at this very moment?

"Mikha'el!" He heard his name and then the hollow blast of a shofar.

He looked up and saw his friend Yochanan[8] hurrying up the path from the wadi, his hair ruffled by the wind and his dark eyes alight with warmth and friendliness, a ram's horn clutched under his arm. Yochanan was always in a hurry, always eager to be first, yet ever a faithful friend. Though Mikha'el was two years older, they had gone to Beth Midrash[9] together in Capernaum. Now, however, Mikha'el didn't see much of his friend. Mikha'el was busy working for his father at the olive press and preparing for his marriage. And when Yochanan

---

8. John
9. A secondary synagogue school at which Jewish boys who had celebrated their bar mitzvahs (at 12 or 13 years of age; the term *bar mitzvah* wasn't used in Jesus' time) could study Torah and the oral traditions of their faith.

wasn't helping with his father's fishing business, he was absorbed in his studies with a local rabbi. Earlier in the year, Yochanan and his teacher had even traveled deep into the wilderness where their Israelite ancestors had wandered.

"Here," said Yochanan, holding out the ram's horn. In ancient times, the Israelites had blown the shofar as a battle cry. Now it was used to announce feasts and festivals and other religious ceremonies. "I've kept this as a surprise. I bought it from a nomad near Hebron on my trip. We can use this to announce that you've arrived in Capernaum to take Elisheva home. The whole town will hear this!"

Mikha'el ran his callused fingers over the intricate carvings in the gray-and-ivory-streaked bone. "Thank you," he said, and he laid the horn carefully in the grass beneath the olive tree, out of the way of his youngest nieces and nephews, who were racing around the walls, playing. "Now," he said with a grin, rubbing his hands together briskly, "want to help me finish this wall?"

"I think I'm better at cleaning fish," Yochanan said with a laugh, "but I'll give it a try. What do you want me to do?"

As the two established a work rhythm, Yochanan shaping the stones with a hammer and Mikha'el setting them in place, they talked about events that had been stirring interest in Capernaum and Korazin. The rabbi Yochanan studied with had been attracting many students with some of his interesting interpretations of the Torah.[10] Still, their conversation inevitably came back to Mikha'el's marriage.

"My mother pointed out your betrothed at the well the other day," Yochanan said. "I knew a bride price had been paid for her, of course, because she was wearing a veil. Elisheva is a fine choice. Her reputation is impeccable, and her family is known for their faithfulness."

"I've been meaning to come down and talk with you about the wedding," said Mikha'el. "I would like you to attend me. You will, won't you?" Mikha'el wanted his best friend to be the one to lead the wedding procession, to stand outside the door and announce the consummation of his marriage to Elisheva and the beginning of the week-long feast.

"Of course," said Yochanan. "I was hoping you'd ask me. You are a fortunate man, my friend. When is the wedding?"

Mikha'el sighed, and when he spoke, his voice betrayed his frustration. "Nobody knows," he said. "Not my mother. Not my brothers. Not even me. I don't think even the angels know. No one knows the hour or the day—only my father."

"As it should be," Yochanan said with a smile, giving Mikha'el a gentle nudge.

---

10. The five books of Moses. The word *Torah* means "teachings," although it's often translated as "law."

"Well, I must be off now. I promised to help mend nets this afternoon." He started quickly down the path, then stopped for a moment and looked back. "The place you're preparing is beautiful, Mikha'el. Your bride will love it."

After Yochanan disappeared from sight, Mikha'el returned to his work. Only a few more courses to go at this corner. Almost finished.

A short time later, as the sun shot a golden glimmer through the gray clouds over the hills, Mikha'el set the last stone in place. Breathing a sigh, he hoped his father would say that at last the time had come for him to claim his bride.

In the same way, after the supper he took the cup, saying, "This cup is the new covenant in my blood, which is poured out for you."
(Luke 22:20)

Do you not know that your body is a temple of the Holy Spirit, who is in you, whom you have received from God? You are not your own; you were bought at a price.

(1 Corinthians 6:19–20a)

When Jesus said, "This cup is the new covenant in My blood," He was saying to us, "I love you. Will you marry Me? Will you be My spiritual bride?"

What an incredible statement! What passionate love Jesus has for His own! The bride price established by God the Father and the cup He offers to seal our relationship with Him are the very lifeblood of the Bridegroom Jesus.

In the Jewish marriage ceremony, the bride could choose to take the cup offered by the bridegroom and drink the wine, or she could refuse. If she took the cup, she accepted the offer of the life of the bridegroom and promised her own in return.

When Jesus offers the cup to us, His chosen bride, He, too, demands a decision and a commitment. Will we give ourselves to Him?

Once we've accepted His offer of marriage and have become the betrothed bride of Jesus, our bride price has been paid—and the cost was our Bridegroom's life.

Our responsibility now is the same as that of the Jewish bride. She spent the time between the betrothal and the marriage ceremony preparing to be the kind of wife who would honor her husband. We, too, are to live in a way that honors our Husband-to-be and prepare ourselves for the day when He will return to take us to His Father's house.

Our sinfulness prevents us from being the perfect bride, but our Bridegroom offers forgiveness. Still, that doesn't lessen our responsibility to live in such a way that when people observe our lives, they know we belong to Him. They know our life commitment is to our Bridegroom.

Even as we prepare ourselves for His coming, however, we need to picture our Bridegroom eagerly working in His Father's house, preparing places for each of us. "In My Father's house are many rooms," Jesus said. "I am going there to prepare a place for you."

The Jewish bridegroom didn't know when he would go to claim his bride. Only his father knew when all the preparations had been made and the time was right.

The engaged bride had no idea when her husband would arrive to claim her; still, she was confident he would come, and as time passed her anticipation grew. She expected the unexpected. Finally, one evening, she would suddenly hear the sound of the shofar in the distance. When she heard that, she knew her bridegroom was coming. Their marriage would soon be consummated, and the wedding feast would begin.

That's where we are today. The bride price has been paid. The cup of the new covenant in His blood has been offered, and we have accepted it. Now we're in the process of preparing ourselves to be the bride of Jesus, even as He is in His Father's house preparing a place for each one of us. And when the Father indicates to the Son that the time is right, our wedding day will arrive. The trumpet will sound, and then we'll join His insula as His bride, His family, together for eternity.

The joy of heaven is both the eternal relationship with our Bridegroom Jesus and the community of His family. (Since we'll have to live together as His community, it might be wise for us to learn to love each other and get along now!)

Our challenge, our call, is to be faithful so that when that day arrives, we're ready to meet our Bridegroom.

> Let us rejoice and be glad
>   and give him glory!
> For the wedding of the Lamb has come,
>   and his bride has made herself ready. . . .
> Blessed are those who are invited to the wedding supper
>   of the Lamb!
>
> (Revelation 19:7,9a)

Chapter 3

The Good Shepherd

The LORD is my shepherd, I shall not be in want.
    He makes me lie down in green pastures,
he leads me beside quiet waters,
    he restores my soul.
He guides me in paths of righteousness
    for his name's sake.
Even though I walk
    through the valley of the shadow of death,
I will fear no evil,
    for you are with me;
your rod and your staff,
    they comfort me.

                    (Psalm 23:1–4)

I am the good shepherd. The good shepherd lays down his life
for the sheep.

                    (John 10:11)

When he saw the crowds, he had compassion on them, because they were harassed and helpless, like sheep without a shepherd.
(Matthew 9:36)

But you, Bethlehem, in the land of Judah,
are by no means least among the rulers of Judah;
for out of you will come a ruler
who will be the shepherd of my people Israel.
(Matthew 2:6)

And there were shepherds living out in the fields nearby, keeping watch over their flocks at night.
(Luke 2:8)

Bethlehem, about 4 B.C.

Rachel wrapped her woolen haluk[1] more closely about her to keep out the wind that blew across the fields. With the winter sun low in the sky, late afternoon could be cool here in the shadows of the Judean Mountains.

Since daybreak, she and her brother Efrayim[2] had been out with the flock, leading them along the centuries-old paths worn into the hillsides around Beit-Lechem.[3] Her brother was still young. He wanted to run and play and let the sheep see to their own grazing. But Rachel knew how dangerous that could be. Sheep were so stupid. If you didn't lead them exactly where they were supposed to go, they wandered off the edges of cliffs or wound up entangled in thickets or stranded at the bottom of a wadi. Still waters were safe, but the deep and dangerous floods that raced down the wadis after rain in the mountains could swiftly, without warning, sweep the animals away.

"Lead the sheep along the path you want them to follow, Efrayim," she kept reminding him. "Don't walk on one path while they're on another. Keep a straight path between you and the sheep. If you don't, they'll wander off the edge or into danger. And Father can't afford to lose any of these animals. We'll need every one for Passover in the spring."

These lambs were destined to be sold and sacrificed at the Temple in Yerushalayim.[4] In the distance, on the highest hill to the north, she imagined she could see the beautiful white and gold columns rising toward heaven and the wide granite steps leading up to the big Huldah Gates. Rachel loved to visit the Temple, but most of their time in Yerushalayim was spent near the Sheep Gate, where the market was located. Passover lambs had to come from the flocks of Beit-Lechem, said the rabbis, and Rachel's family was one of the many Levite families who provided this service. Her father was an honest dealer, however,

---

1. Outer garment
2. Ephraim
3. Bethlehem
4. Jerusalem

unlike some of the others. She had overheard her parents talking about the dishonest Levitical families who sold imperfect lambs or resold animals that had already been rejected by the priests. Some of the Sadducees who ran the Temple also cheated the people.

"All they care about is making money," her father said. They had even expanded the Temple market into the Court of the Gentiles[5] during feast days, her father said angrily. "They have taken away the Gentiles' place of prayer," he growled.

Rachel looked back at the flock following her now. Lowering their soft, blunt faces, the sheep nipped off the tiny, green shoots of grass that had sprung up among the rocks since she had last brought them this way.

How trusting they are, she thought. *I could lead them anywhere and they would follow my voice.* How helpless they were without her. If the leopards and jackals had their way, only bones would be left on the hillside.

Making sure the lambs didn't fall from the precarious paths and finding them the best tufts of grass wasn't easy. And how hard she had to work to move these animals from one tuft to another!

Father calls this the green pastures, she thought. Yet the grass grew up through the rocky soil in such tiny clumps that she had to constantly lead the animals to a fresh grazing spot. From a distance, the land looked like a garden of rocks, without any green or growing thing. Up close, however, the tiny sprigs of life were everywhere.

Suddenly, she noticed one of the spring lambs wandering off around the corner of the hill. "Little Trouble," she called this one. He was ornery, stubborn, and always nosing his way into thickets or some kind of trouble.

"Efrayim," she called. "Watch the herd while I fetch Little Trouble."

Rachel hurried across the field, keeping her eye on the lamb, which was determinedly heading toward a thicket perched on a precarious ledge. The waterskin tied to her sash slapped against her thigh as she ran. She had to reach the lamb before he tumbled to the wadi below. Thinking only of his hunger, the animal could easily and quickly fall to his death—or, at the very least, serious harm.

Just before Little Trouble got to the thicket, he stopped abruptly at a patch of grass and began nibbling. Relieved but wary of the dangerously close precipice, Rachel edged her way to the lamb and scooped him up in her arms. As she carried Little Trouble back to the flock, she scolded him gently.

---

5. The place where Gentiles were allowed to gather and pray by the Temple in Jerusalem. (See Temple diagram on p. 157.)

Rachel was proud of her shepherding skills, and she loved the freedom of the sun, the wind, and the open spaces. Gazing at the brown Judean Mountains to the east, she sometimes imagined what it would be like to explore their mysterious canyons, searching the caves in the cliffs or looking for the hidden waterfalls of a desert oasis. In another year, as she approached marriageable age, she would have to begin staying home more to learn household skills from her mother. But for now she was thankful her father needed her help in the fields.

She watched Efrayim as he tugged a lamb away from a thicket before its wool tangled. Her older brother, Yosef,[6] who studied with a rabbi during the day, seldom helped with the sheep now. But her father would soon be out to take the night watch with her. Her youngest brother, only two months old, was still just a tiny form swaddled in strips of cloth. He felt so soft when she cuddled him against her.

A sharp gust of wind cut across the hillside, and she noticed the lengthening shadows. Rosy swatches from the setting sun streaked the sky. She could see the first star.

"Efrayim," she called, "we need to round them up for the night." She wanted to get the animals off the hillside before nightfall. Sheep were more prone to wander in the dark.

"Remember to stay with the flock now," she reminded her brother. This was the time when a good shepherd dropped back among the sheep, walking with them down into the valley shadows. "They need to see you, to feel you with them. They must hear your voice."

"Rachel," her brother called just then, "what's happening up on the mountain?"

"The mountain" was what she and Efrayim called the ominous fortress looming above them. Though it was five miles south of Beit-Lechem, the cone-shaped outline of its mountain base filled the horizon. The huge, round eastern tower of the fortress on top stuck high into the sky. This palace-stronghold belonged to the king of their land, Herod the Great.

As she stared up at the mountain, Rachel could almost feel the king and his guards looking down on them. Although Herod's soldiers seldom bothered the people in her village, their presence kept fear alive in everyone's hearts.

At the foot of the mountain was an enormous palace and storehouses, as well as a huge pool of water surrounded by beautiful gardens and tall, white, marble columns. People said the king loved to swim, and the pool was large enough that he and his guests could sail or row small boats on it. Even those who hated the ruler admired the way he had moved an entire mountain of earth here to form

---

6. Joseph

Herod's Mountain. Herod built his great fortress of Herodion on a hill near Bethlehem. The huge, circular structure was surrounded with earth, creating a man-made mountain visible for miles. The fortress extended three stories above the cone. (*Ray Vander Laan*)

the foundation for his fortress. "If you have Herod's vision, you can move mountains," her father liked to joke.

"Look, Rachel!" Efrayim said. "See all the torches moving around up there? What do you think they're doing?"

"Maybe they're getting ready to leave for the winter," Rachel said. Her parents had told her that each winter the king moved to another palace at Yericho,[7] where the climate was much warmer.

"Never mind that now, Efrayim," she said. "It's time for you to go home and get your supper." Since Efrayim was still so young, he didn't stay out overnight with the flock.

Other shepherds, many of them boys and girls her age, were leading their flocks toward the cluster of small, stone-walled pens huddled together in the field below. By the time she had driven her sheep into the fold, the sky was dark.

Rachel spread her bedroll across the entrance and settled herself against the

---

7. Jericho

rough comfort of the ancient stone wall. On guard, she kept the animals in and the predators out. When her father came, he would bring fresh bread and cheese for her supper, and they would build a small fire to keep warm.

Rachel sat in the darkness, listening to the distant voices of the other shepherds and watching the stars blink on. One appeared to shine brighter than the rest. It seemed closer somehow. She watched it for a long time.

For many years when I read Psalm 23 or the other shepherd images in Scripture, including those used by Jesus Himself, I pictured the shepherd driving the sheep into lush, green fields of alfalfa. I was wrong. Shepherds in Israel don't drive the sheep; they *lead* them along the narrow paths that still crisscross the Judean hillsides. "This is the way to go," the shepherd says to the sheep. "Follow me."

And the green pastures of Israel are not belly-deep alfalfa; they're sparse tufts of grass springing up in a sometimes unbelievably rocky landscape. From one moment to the next, the sheep depend on the leading of the shepherd and the sufficiency of the grazing he provides.

When we understand the shepherd and the land out of which Jesus' imagery comes, the meaning of His words becomes clearer. "I am the good Shepherd. I am out there ahead of you. This is the way to go. This is the way to live. Follow Me."

We're not to wait to be driven, to be forced to move along a certain path. Nor are we to wait until we're lost or stuck in some dangerous place. Rather, we are, through life, to follow the ways laid out by the Shepherd, to follow in His footsteps and the example He has set for us. Straight paths or paths of righteousness—the paths the Shepherd selects—are the only ones that are safe and secure.

"No matter how difficult, how narrow, or how treacherous the path, I've walked it first," says Jesus. "I always go before My sheep."

Picturing God's green pastures as rich Iowa farmland where everything we need for the rest of our lives is close at hand destroys the vibrancy of Christian living. Not one of us knows for sure that we have what it takes to deal with what will happen to us a few days from now—or even a few minutes from now—any more than the sheep have the grass to satisfy the hunger of tomorrow. All we have is what's sufficient for this moment. With that knowledge, we can relax, relying on the effectiveness of our Shepherd to provide whatever we need in the future.

Thus, it's incredibly important to keep our eyes on Him, because the green pastures 10 minutes from now or tomorrow or next week are only available if we follow Him. Without Him, we'll starve. We'll lose our way. We need to learn to live for each moment, trusting and depending on God for whatever lies ahead.

Worry, on the other hand, means trying to deal with tomorrow's problems in today's pastures. Living the Christian life is a moment-by-moment event as we seek the provision of God each step of the way.

There's good reason for this. Like sheep, we can't distinguish the dangerous cliff from the safe path or the deadly floodwaters of the wadi from the quiet pool. Only the Shepherd can lead us safely away from the water that destroys and toward the refreshing water that gives life.

We are, by nature, emotionally and spiritually hungry and thirsty people. We long to be important, to be fulfilled, to make life meaningful. Those are God-given yearnings. Unfortunately, we often take the wrong way. We seek satisfaction in things that may look hunger-satisfying and thirst-quenching but are, in fact, deadly. Trusting our own senses and desires, we wander into places that can destroy our character, our potential, and even our lives. When we listen to the Shepherd, however, we're kept from danger.

Although Jesus is always the Shepherd, He allows others to care for His sheep. Thus, we find His leading not only in His Word, but also through the voices of His undershepherds: pastors and teachers, parents and family, and godly friends. Through them, *He* leads us to the green pastures and quiet waters.

The shepherd isn't always out in front, leading his sheep, however. As the sun sets on the Judean hills, with their confused tangle of trails, steep cliffs, and deep wadis, it becomes increasingly difficult for the sheep to follow the shepherd and increasingly likely that they may misstep, fall, or get lost. Then, in the lengthening twilight, when the sheep must pass through the darkest shadows in the deepest wadis, the shepherd drops back and walks *with* them.

When those moments arrive for us—when we lose a beloved parent, spouse, or child; when we face pain or suffering; when we wake in the middle of the night fearing the unknown; or even in the midst of a particularly hard day at work—we, too, need to search out the Shepherd's presence. We need the immediacy of His comfort, the strengthening sound of His voice, and the protection of His presence.

> *Even though I walk through the valley of the shadow of death,*
> *I will fear no evil, for you are with me.*
>
> (Psalm 23:4)

Jesus, our Passover Lamb, born among the flocks of Bethlehem and visited by the Bethlehem shepherds, understands well what it means to be a strong, faithful shepherd.

It's interesting that the Lord chose to announce His Son's birth to shepherds in the fields of Bethlehem. Do you suppose it was because they, of all people, would understand the importance of listening to and obeying the Shepherd's voice?

Will you follow His voice wherever He leads?

Chapter 4

The King

Isaac prayed to the LORD on behalf of his wife, because she was barren. The LORD answered his prayer, and his wife Rebekah became pregnant. The babies jostled each other within her, and she said, "Why is this happening to me?" So she went to inquire of the LORD.

The LORD said to her,
"Two nations are in your womb,
and two peoples from within you will be separated;
one people will be stronger than the other,
and the older will serve the younger."

When the time came for her to give birth, there were twin boys in her womb. The first to come out was . . . Esau. After this, his brother came out, with his hand grasping Esau's heel; so he was named Jacob.

(Genesis 25:21–26a)

Esau said to his father, "Do you have only one blessing, my father? Bless me too, my father!" Then Esau wept aloud.

His father Isaac answered him . . . "You will live by the sword and you will serve your brother." . . .

This was Esau the father of the Edomites.

(Genesis 27:38–40; 36:43b)

A star will come out of Jacob;
   a scepter will rise out of Israel.
He will crush the foreheads of Moab. . . .
   Edom will be conquered . . .
but Israel will grow strong.
   A ruler will come out of Jacob.

(Numbers 24:17b–19)

"The house of Jacob will be a fire
and the house of Joseph a flame;
the house of Esau will be stubble,
and they will set it on fire and consume it.
There will be no survivors
from the house of Esau." The LORD has spoken.

(Obadiah 18)

After this, Jesus traveled about from one town and village to another, proclaiming the good news of the kingdom of God. The Twelve were with him, and also some women . . . Mary (called Magdalene) . . . Joanna the wife of Cuza, the manager of Herod's household . . . and many others. These women were helping to support them out of their own means.

(Luke 8:1–3)

Herodion, near Bethlehem, about 4 B.C.

Sixty-eight, 69, 70. Yochanah[1] counted the carved, white, marble stair treads as she climbed.

Seventy-one, 72, 73. She did it out of habit now.

Seventy-four, 75, 76. When she reached 100, she would be halfway.

That old fox Herod was always looking over his shoulder. Why else would he build this oppressively dark passageway up to his fortress on top of the mountain overlooking the Judean countryside? The oil lamps flickering in the niches in the stone walls provided just enough light to keep her from stumbling on the slippery marble.

Always marble, she thought. *Limestone isn't good enough. Herod builds as if he thinks these stones will last forever.*

At least today she'd been able to escape this place for a few hours to visit with her friend Tavita[2] in the nearby village of Beit-Lechem.[3] Over a lunch of barley bread and new wine from the neighboring vineyard, Tavita had told her about interesting stirrings in this out-of-the-way place.

Beit-Lechem, a small community of shepherds and farmers, with its olive trees and vineyards climbing the hillsides, was usually quiet. It was far enough beyond the Judean hills to be green and far enough from Herod to be out of his mind most of the time.

Though she served in Herod's household, Yochanah was often troubled by the fact that this Edomite lived and ruled in the very place where the great king Daveed[4] was born. She wasn't old enough to remember the days of the Maccabees, but she knew her people's history well. Her father and grandfather had told her the bloody tales: how Herod had seized the throne from the house of the Maccabees; how he had married the niece of the very Maccabean ruler he

---

1. Joanna
2. Tabitha
3. Bethlehem
4. David

had supplanted so he might ingratiate himself with the Jews; and how he'd had her killed a few years later—as he had most of the Hasmonaean aristocracy.

Prompted by something her friend said, Yochanah had been thinking about this as she and Tavita ate lunch.

"Yochanah?" Her friend had to call her back from her musings.

"I'm sorry—what were you saying?"

Tavita continued telling of a recent strange incident in the village. A couple had come to Beit-Lechem for the census, she said, and while there, the young wife had given birth.

"It's been such a madhouse lately with all the people coming to report for this stupid census," said Tavita. "Every lodging place for miles around has been taken. But this man and his wife had traveled all the way down from Natzeret,[5] and in her condition, there was no way they could make it back the six miles to Yerushalayim [6] to look for lodging. So my neighbor offered them a place in his stable."

"She had the baby there?" Yochanah asked, pointing to the stable built against the hillside under Tavita's house. Every home had such a shelter for its animals.

Tavita shrugged. "Well, it was warm and dry. And the birth went fine," she said. "Then the strange part happened.

"That same night some of the local shepherds came around to several houses—came here, in fact—asking if we knew anything about a baby boy being born. They said they had been told he was the Messiah. I hear that when they finally found this couple, all the shepherds crowded into the stable to see their baby."

"That *is* strange," said Yochanah. "Of course, everyone hates the Romans. We're all looking for a deliverer. But how could this child be Messiah while the Edomite is still king? Didn't the prophet say that Ya'akov [7] would rule over Esav [8]?" *And hadn't other self-proclaimed messiahs only brought more bloodshed?* she thought.

"True," said Tavita. "But since that night, these shepherds have been going around telling people how they saw a heavenly vision that told them to go look for this child in a manger. And that's where they found him."

What Yochanah hadn't dared tell her friend, what she thought about now as she climbed back up to the Herodion, was that she had already heard about this

---

5. Nazareth
6. Jerusalem
7. Jacob
8. Esau

baby. But if the king or his spies knew she had spoken of what she had over-heard, her indiscretion could cost her life.

First Yochanah's husband had told her how upset the king was. "About some baby born in Beit-Lechem," Cuza said. "He's gotten it into his head that this is another threat to his throne. He sees plots around every corner." As Herod's steward, in charge of his finances, Cuza was privy to many of the king's private conversations.

Then Yochanah herself had observed the king's disturbed demeanor. Since she oversaw all the menus and dining arrangements in Herod's household, Yochanah was often present when he had guests. This had been the case two days ago when the king entertained several visitors in the colonnaded triclineum. The sky had been clear azure above the king's indoor garden that day as she made her way around the water fountain and along the marble pathway among the palm and fruit trees. The green marble tray she carried was heavy with figs and dates. Its handles, carved into the shape of grapevines, cut into her hands.

As she stepped into the dining area where the king and his guests reclined on the ornate couches, she heard Herod laughingly refer to some child in Beit-Lechem who was "born to be king of the Jews!" His thick fingers with their heavy rings clasped and unclasped as he told them he'd been to Yerushalayim to meet with the Sadducees about the matter. "I thought I ought to let them know they might have a little competition," he said with a laugh.

Yochanah recognized the paranoia under his sarcasm, and it made her shiver with fear. In such a mood, he was capable of anything. Hadn't he murdered his own wife, Mariamme, and his sons Alexander and Aristobulus? He was a good ruler, it was true. His building programs provided steady jobs for thousands. And when famine or other calamities threatened any of his subjects, he freely provided clothing and grain from his storehouses. But those occasions were eclipsed by his vicious tyranny and paranoia.

Thankfully, it was almost time for him to move to his palace at Yericho[9] for the winter. That day couldn't come soon enough for her. He was always in a better mood when he first made his seasonal moves.

Yochanah and Cuza were part of the staff who moved with the king from place to place. She enjoyed seeing his many beautiful palaces with their marble columns, rich mosaics, hot and cold baths, and swimming pools—everywhere swimming pools. But whenever they returned here to the Herodion, this strong-hold Herod had named after himself, she grew depressed. As a child, she had

---

9. Jericho

been taught by her father, an elder in their village synagogue, that the Messiah would come from this place. Hadn't the prophet Micah foretold:

> But you, Beit-Lechem Ephrathah,
>> though you are small among the clans of Y'hudah,[10]
> out of you will come for me
>> one who will be ruler over Israel,
> whose origins are from of old,
>> from ancient times.[11]

Yet as long as Herod, from the line of Esav, ruled over this place and all of Judea, how could Messiah come?

From the tower window in his private quarters, Herod gazed southwest toward the misty, red mountains of his homeland of Edom, beyond the Salt Sea.[12] Of all his fortresses, he felt safest here. Masada, deep in the Judean Wilderness to the south, was more isolated and unapproachable, but from here he could see every strategic point of the compass. To the south the mountains of Hebron, to the east the Judean Mountains and Wilderness, and to the north the city of Yerushalayim. Below him, the fields were dotted not with enemy encampments but with flocks of sheep. He looked down on the small, scattered villages. One of them in particular drew his attention.

Beit-Lechem! How could such a ramshackle little place give him so much trouble?

These Jews! Every baby boy was a possible messiah. They were obsessed with the subject, forever talking about this messiah of theirs. A more troublesome people he had never seen. The Temple forces and their greedy ambition for power meant he always had to watch his back.

Still, he could handle them. And he was very good at watching his back. His network of informers had drawn in many enemies and enabled him to forestall various factions.

The sword was the only voice these Jews understood. Gallus, captain of his garrison here, could set his soldiers to work at a moment's notice, and his crucifixion squads were an effective way of keeping the peace. The sword and the cross were powerful deterrents.

---

10. Judah
11. Micah 5:2
12. Dead Sea

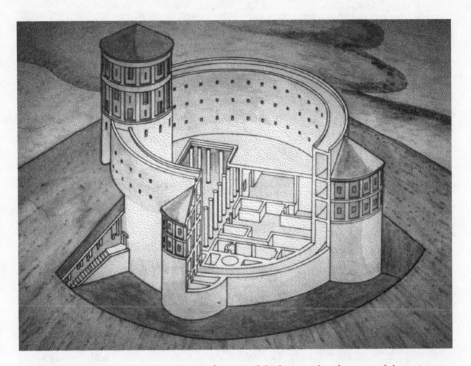

Herod's Magnificent Palace. The Herodion was one of the largest palace-fortresses of the ancient world. The upper fortress included a garden with a colonnade, a magnificent dining hall, and a Roman bath. The eastern tower was over six stories high. (*Leen Ritmeyer*)

Even his wife and sons had betrayed him. Though the marriage had been politically expedient, he had loved beautiful Mariamme more than his other nine wives. Had she really conspired against him? Sometimes late at night, the haunting dreams of her last breath being strangled from her body made him wonder. No. In the light of day, he knew she had proved herself as traitorous as the rest of her family, just as her treacherous Hasmonaean blood in the veins of his two sons had flowed out in their lies and plots. They had followed their mother's ways. Fortunately, they had all underestimated his power and network of spies.

But you, Beit-Lechem . . . out of you will come one who will be ruler over Israel.

The words of the Jewish prophet haunted him also, and he couldn't get this Beit-Lechem matter out of his mind. Not the rumors. The rumors would die out on their own. After all, what was another messiah? It was the recent visit from those Babylonian stargazers that troubled him. He didn't believe such soothsayers. Just to be safe, however, he'd met with the chief priests and teachers at the Temple in Yerushalayim. They'd been no help at all, other than confirming what he already knew: The Hebrew prophets had said that their Messiah, a descendant of Ya'akov, would be born in Beit-Lechem.

While in Yerushalayim, he had also conferred with his foreman about the Temple renovations. The new Temple was completed. Now work was progressing well on its colonnaded courts. It was another of his architectural masterpieces. When the Jews saw how he was refurbishing their religious center, they would be ecstatic. Maybe that would get them off his back once and for all.

The house of Ya'akov will be a fire . . . and the house of Yosef[13] *a flame; the house of Esav will be stubble.*

Suddenly, a sharp pain lanced through his lower body. He doubled over in agony. Though it subsided as quickly as it came, it left a dull ache. He summoned a servant to bring him a cup of wine. Its warmth soothed him as he drank, but soon a sharp acid taste filled his mouth. Another stomach upset from worrying over all these problems.

Why he troubled himself about some peasant baby, he didn't know. Wasn't he Herod, the greatest builder the world had ever known? He had moved mountains and reclaimed the sea—achieved architectural wonders to rival Egypt and Rome. Look at his gem of a palace and magnificent harbor at Caesarea. White marble against the turquoise Mediterranean. And his palaces at Yericho and Masada. His vast cisterns . . . aqueducts . . . pools . . . baths. And now the Temple. Long after his enemies were dust, his name and works would survive, glorious testimonies to his brilliance.

Still . . .

The Hebrew Bible promised that the descendants of Ya'akov would overpower the descendants of Esav, the forefather of his people. What foolishness! For centuries, these insane Jews had been stealing other people's cities, usurping other people's power. He was proud of his heritage and his beautiful Arabian mother.

His accomplishments were world famous. He had even devised a trademark design for his building stones. He rubbed his hand over the limestone blocks, delighting in the chiseled margin that bordered each stone. Herod's stones, they called them. Armies of slaves had cut thousands of these for his buildings at Yericho, Caesarea, and Yerushalayim. He touched the smooth marble ledge before him, his favorite white marble with gray swirls through it. The sight and feel of its cool elegance always soothed him.

He became uneasy again, however, as his gaze settled on the wall that had

---

13. Joseph

Herodian Stones. These large stones are part of Herod's wall of the Temple Mount in Jerusalem. The edges of each stone (called margins) are cut so the center (called boss) protrudes, creating the distinctive Herodian style. The largest of these stones weigh over 500 tons. The groove in the stones was cut much later. (*Ray Vander Laan*)

once boasted an ornate mirror with a gold-and-ivory-inlaid frame. He'd had it removed. He could no longer bear to look at his image. His athletic and robust body was wasting away. Although he swam each day and enjoyed the warm sun, his color wasn't good. Just a stomach disorder, his doctors said. Still . . .

There will be no survivors from the house of Esav. The Lord has spoken. So the Jewish prophet had written.

Once more Herod gazed toward the east, then turned to look down at the village of Beit-Lechem to the north and toward the high hills of Yerushalayim beyond. Maybe he needed to take matters in hand . . . *no survivors* . . . just in case.

He called for the guard outside the chamber door. "Tell your captain I want to see him immediately," he ordered.

Minutes later, when Gallus appeared, Herod commanded, "Ready a squad of soldiers! I have a job for them!"

The Jewish shepherds to whom the angels announced Jesus' birth faced a dilemma from the outset. Deep within their religious tradition, passed from generation to generation, was the prophecy that the Messiah would be a descendant of Jacob, whose line represented those God had chosen to be His own. This Messiah, the prophecy said, would rule over the descendants of Esau, the Edomite whose line represented those who had chosen the way of the evil one. For the Jew, *Esau* and *Edom* were synonyms for evil.

Yet, here were God's messengers announcing that the Messiah had been born in the shadow of the Herodion, a symbol of the might and power of the greatest descendant of Esau who had ever lived—Herod the Great.

The angels were challenging the shepherds to make a commitment based not on appearance but on trust in the faithfulness of God. They were saying to them, "Will you believe that regardless of how powerful Herod appears to be—regardless of how great his fortresses, how extensive his influence, and how pervasive his evil—he is not the king? Will you believe that the descendants of Esau are not in control and that evil has not won the day? Will you trust that in God's plan, what appears to be is not? Will you believe that this baby born in a humble manger is the true King, Lord of heaven and earth, through whose weakness the strength of Almighty God will be seen?"

Today, the power of evil and those who follow its ways is as compelling as ever. The influence of those who have chosen to live apart from God's direction is pervasive. To outward appearances, evil infects everything in our culture: media, advertising, publishing, science, education.

As modern followers of Jesus, we're given the same challenge the Jewish shepherds received centuries ago: "Will you believe that the One who is truly King, seated at God's right hand in heaven, is the One who appears weak and not strong? Will you trust God's Word and not your own perceptions?"

We must not be taken in by appearances of power: the entertainment moguls in Hollywood; the high-finance and advertising executives on Wall Street and

Madison Avenue; the bigots who espouse racial division and violence; the drug lords; the terrorists who kill innocent children. All that evil power will someday be utterly destroyed.

As Jesus' followers, we must believe in and be completely committed to His kingship, based not on appearance but on faith in what He has told us. Following Him, becoming part of His kingdom, is the only way to be on God's side in the struggle for the minds and lives of those in our culture.

The disciples discovered this. By trusting Jesus and committing themselves to apparent weakness, they aligned themselves with the greatest Power in the universe. As a result, their lives and ministry turned the world upside down.

When we commit ourselves to the true King, we, too, can bring about changes that shake and shape our world. We can make an immeasurable difference in our classrooms, our offices, our factories—wherever we happen to be.

Even though the cultural and political descendants of Herod still seem dominant, Jesus of Nazareth is really in control. No matter what it looks like, the devil isn't in charge. We have to believe that fact if we're to find the courage to confront the world and make a difference for Him.

Herod the Great left his marble palaces and millions of tons of huge stones—quarried, chiseled with his distinctive ornamentation, and set into magnificent buildings. Jesus of Nazareth left "living stones," spread around the world.

Today, Herod's kingdom lies broken and scattered beneath sea and earth.

Jesus' kingdom, on the other hand, will stand forever.

Part 2

How He Taught

Chapter 5

The Rabbi

Jesus returned to Galilee in the power of the Spirit, and news about him spread through the whole countryside. He taught in their synagogues, and everyone praised him.

He went to Nazareth, where he had been brought up, and on the Sabbath day he went into the synagogue, as was his custom. And he stood up to read. The scroll of the prophet Isaiah was handed to him. Unrolling it, he found the place where it is written:

"The Spirit of the Lord is on me,
    because he has anointed me
    to preach good news to the poor.
He has sent me to proclaim freedom for the prisoners
    and recovery of sight for the blind,
    to release the oppressed,
    to proclaim the year of the Lord's favor."

Then he rolled up the scroll, gave it back to the attendant and sat down. The eyes of everyone in the synagogue were fastened on him, and he began by saying to them, "Today this scripture is fulfilled in your hearing."

(Luke 4:14–21)

When Jesus had finished saying these things, the crowds were amazed at his teaching, because he taught as one who had authority, and not as their teachers of the law.

(Matthew 7:28–29)

Come to me, all you who are weary and burdened, and I will give you rest. Take my yoke upon you and learn from me, for I am gentle and humble in heart, and you will find rest for your souls. For my yoke is easy and my burden is light.

(Matthew 11:28–30)

Then Jesus said to the crowds and to his disciples: "The teachers of the law and the Pharisees sit in Moses' seat. So you must obey them and do everything they tell you. But do not do what they do, for they do not practice what they preach. They tie up heavy loads and put them on men's shoulders, but they themselves are not willing to lift a finger to move them."

(Matthew 23:1–4)

Nazareth, A.D. 68

wo walls were still standing, stained with a frieze of flame-shaped black streaks from the enemies' fires. The rest of the synagogue had been smashed and toppled. The tenth legion had done its work effectively.

The old man's heart wept as he gazed at the huge pieces of fallen limestone. His finger shakily traced a carving of the menorah[1] on one of the shattered columns.

This house of prayer has been my home for over 50 years, Shmu'el[2] thought.

His legs trembled as his foot slipped on a pile of rubble. The Roman soldiers had even pried up some of the paving stones.

They would have destroyed me, too, if they didn't consider me so worthless.

"Get out of here, old man," the stocky captain with the scarred face had ordered. "Thank the gods that you are too old to be of use."

Now Shmu'el was torn between relief and guilt—relief at being spared slavery or death; guilt that he was not sharing the agony of the men, women, and children still huddled in the town square while their fate was decided. The slave markets of Damascus. The galleys. The arena. Death.

The Jews of Natzeret[3] were not alone in their suffering. With this latest Roman crackdown, an attempt to quash the growing Jewish rebellion, the entire land was in turmoil. For years things had been going from bad to worse. Now it seemed the worst had arrived.

Since he was a child, Shmu'el had seen Rome's puppets come and go. Like the Herods. Eager to extend their political power and territory, those usurpers had faithfully fostered the pagan Hellenism that was so offensive to the Jewish community. And the Roman procurators. Fourteen of them since he was a boy. Most served only three or four years, and many were corrupt. The one who had stayed in power the longest, cold and greedy Pontius Pilate, had not only

---

1. A seven-branched candlestick
2. Samuel
3. Nazareth

ravaged the Temple treasury for his public works, but had also tauntingly minted coins bearing pagan symbols, a great offense to the people of Judea.

Rome might be far away in miles, but it was always as close as its legions and governors. And the power of the emperors had grown more vicious with the passing years. One of the worst emperors was the current one, the sadistic Nero, with his insane plots and his tyrannical cult of emperor worship.

Nothing Rome had done, however, by decree or sword, could stop the Jews from resisting and eventually openly rebelling against the plague of pagan practices and oppression that had desecrated their land. Rome, with its pantheon of gods and goddesses, its barbaric games and licentious theater, had continually thrown fresh tinder on the fires of revolution burning in the blood of its conquered subjects. Now those fires blazed high.

Year after year, the Zealot movement, headquartered in the mountain stronghold at Gamla, produced its fierce and fiery brand of insurrectionists. Two of the most brutal were its present leaders, Menachem and El'azar,[4] grandsons of Y'huda,[5] founder of the movement. Even now, rumors said, they were fortifying the walls of their mountaintop city northeast of Gennesaret.[6] Meanwhile, their guerrilla bands used every opportunity to terrorize the Romans—and even their own people.

"Fight fire with fire," they said. "Knife against sword. The Torah[7] says an eye for an eye. We bow our knee to no man. We worship no pagan gods or idols. Slavery is worse than death."

Shmu'el had debated with many of these intransigent individuals over the years, questioning their dedication to violence as well as their refusal to pay taxes. "There's a greater freedom than freedom from oppression," Shmu'el told them.

But they never listened. They reduced every issue to freedom from Rome. Even their own religious feasts had become nothing more than an opportunity to display their rebellion. Every Passover, it seemed, there was an incident in Yerushalayim[8] as the Zealots used that great celebration and its attendant crowds to stir up resistance to the Romans. Since the victory of the Maccabees over the pagans, palm branches waved in the Temple on Sukkot[9] had become a symbol of the Zealots' political defiance.

---

4. Eleazar
5. Judah
6. The Sea of Galilee; also known as the Sea of Tiberias after Herod Antipas's capital city, Tiberias, which he named for his friend the emperor Tiberius.
7. The five books of Moses. The word *Torah* means "teachings," although it's often translated as "law."
8. Jerusalem
9. Also known as the Feast of Tabernacles or Booths. It took place in late fall.

The Synagogue Ruins of Gamla. This synagogue, the oldest found in Israel, was being used when Jesus taught in the area near the city of the Zealots. (*Ray Vander Laan*)

Shmu'el couldn't fault their bravery, if one could call it that. They were fearless. They assassinated people in broad daylight. They boldly mingled with the crowds during festivals, concealing daggers under their clothing. They had even killed the high priest Yochanan[10] because of his sympathy for Rome.

As a result of these terrorist activities, however, the Roman armies were now destroying Shmu'el's land and people. The smoke of their fires singed every breath he took, and their crucifixion poles rose everywhere on the horizon.

Where's their freedom now? Shmu'el wondered.

Suddenly, one of the overturned stones caught his eye. The rough lines of its carving depicted the ark of the covenant.

How many years had it been since the ark was lost? Over 600 years—ever since his ancestors had been carried off to Babylon.

This carving was a reminder that the ark had been the presence of God with Israel, like the pillar of fire and smoke during the desert wanderings.

I, too, have known the presence of Jahweh, Shmu'el thought. He knew it when

10. Jonathan

he unrolled the parchments in the synagogue and read the words Jahweh had given Moshe.[11] He felt it when he walked the fields with his students and saw the truth in the world the Almighty had created. And he especially knew it when he entered the Temple at Yerushalayim on Yom Kippur, that most holy of all days, when the high priest transferred the sins of the people to the head of the goat tethered by a scarlet cord to the gate of the priests' court.

The scapegoat was taken out into the desert to die, but the scarlet cord remained tied to the Temple door. As the days passed and the people watched the cord bleach white in the sun and weather, the Levitical choir would sing the words of Yesha'yahu[12] the prophet:

> *Though your sins are like scarlet,*
> *　　they shall be as white as snow;*
> *though they are red as crimson,*
> *　　they shall be like wool.*[13]

On that yearly day of atonement, more than at any other time, Shmu'el felt the presence of the Almighty, who had made covenant with His people: as the priest put the knife to the lamb's throat; as the scapegoat was led out; as the people's sins were covered with the shedding of blood and removed from the community. That very sense of God's presence at his first Passover, when he was 12, had made Shmu'el want to become a teacher of the Law himself.

Knowing that choosing the rabbi who would teach him was one of the most important things he would ever do, Shmu'el had visited the synagogues in the towns around Natzeret to hear their rabbis teach. He had also listened to the itinerant teachers who passed through Galilee from time to time.

"Why do you do this?" one of his friends had asked. "Isn't our rabbi in Natzeret good enough?"

"I must choose wisely," Shmu'el had told him. "Studying with a rabbi is more than just learning to interpret the Torah. It is something much greater than getting a good education. A talmid[14] must become like his rabbi. So whoever I choose as my master will affect the rest of my life."

Eventually, he had decided to take the yoke of Rabbi Gamaliel in Yerushalayim.

---

11. Moses
12. Isaiah
13. Isaiah 1:18
14. (pl. talmidim) A disciple or student of a rabbi whose desire was not only to know what his teacher knew but also to become like him.

The yoke of Torah, Shmu'el thought. *How heavily it weighs.*

Suddenly, he heard leather-soled boots grinding against rock outside the porch of the synagogue. *Soldiers? Are they coming to get me after all?*

Shmu'el stopped breathing for a moment. Then carefully, quietly, he stepped across the floor toward the back wall. He took a few more steps and stopped, not daring to breathe.

He could hear voices, loud arguing. They didn't seem to be coming closer, but he crept around the corner and into a small, square room with stone benches on all four walls. No damage. The soldiers must have tired of their game before they got here.

Shmu'el sank onto the nearest bench, leaned back against the hard, cool, block wall, and whooshed out his breath. His armpits were wet beneath his haluk[15] and prayer shawl.

Following the custom, he pulled his prayer shawl over his head, creating his own prayer chamber, closed his eyes, and began with the traditional blessing and praise of Jahweh.

"Blessed are you, O Lord our God, King of the universe, who gives courage to the fearful. Help me, O Father of Avraham.[16] May I not fear the shadow of death."

How many times had he taught his own talmidim the rabbinical teaching based on Yesha'yahu the prophet? "Why are you afraid, O you of little faith? Didn't Jahweh say 'I am with you'?"[17]

The sun coming through the open roof was warm against Shmu'el's eyelids. His hands rested at his sides against the smooth limestone. The tekton's[18] chisel marks had been worn away by years of students sitting on these benches. In the stillness, Shmu'el could hear the echo of young, clear voices reciting the Torah. In his mind, their childish voices changed and deepened, and their answers became questions as they debated interpretations of the Law with their teacher.

Shmu'el thought of his own years in synagogue school here and how excited he had been when he went to Yerushalayim to begin his advanced studies with Rabbi Gamaliel. In fact, he still remembered the first day the rabbi led them out of the synagogue and into the countryside beyond the city walls, through the fields and surrounding towns, where they began to learn how to live in obedi-

---

15. Outer garment
16. Abraham
17. Isaiah 41:10
18. A stonemason or builder; sometimes translated as "carpenter."

ence to Torah—how to become like their rabbi. He still thought of that as the first day they went out to study life.

Out to face life. That's what he had to do now. He couldn't cower here.

Shmu'el walked back into the main room of the synagogue. Most of the benches had been crushed under fallen columns of stone, but Moshe's seat was still partly intact. The inscription around the base, commemorating the benefactor who had paid the stonemason to carve it, could still be read clearly: *Remember for good, Y'hudah, son of Y'hoshua,*[19] *who provided this . . .*

On Shabbat,[20] any member of the community could, when it was his turn, read from the five books given to Moshe on Sinai. What an honor it was to sit at the front of the synagogue on the broad, smooth limestone of Moshe's seat and read from the soft parchment scroll with its carefully copied characters! To actually hold the Word of Jahweh in his hands!

This synagogue had been a place of prayer, a community center, for more than 100 years. Would the Romans ever let them rebuild it? Even if they did, Shmu'el thought, he was too old to see the restoration of this place where he had known the presence of God.

He still remembered one of those times, almost 40 years ago. He could remember how the air felt that day and how the sky looked.

Nazareth, A.D. 28

uge, puffy, lamb's wool clouds carpeted the blue-gray sky. The winter rains were still a couple of months off, so the air was brittle with dust. The green of spring had turned sere and brown months ago.

As he trudged up the rocky path to the synagogue, Shmu'el looked out across the fertile plain of the Jezreel Valley to the west of Natzeret. Even that looked brown and dry. To the north of the plain rose the huge fortified city of Meggido. Some called the entire valley Har-Meggido[21] because of the countless battles that had been fought there over the centuries.

Whoever controlled Meggido controlled the great trade route that some called the Via Maris.[22] This road ran along the eastern edge of the Mediterranean, linking Egypt and the lands to the east, north, and west. Some rabbis taught that

---

19. Joshua
20. The Sabbath. It began at sundown on Friday night and ended at sundown on Saturday night.
21. Means "mound" or "tel" of Meggido; also known as Armageddon.
22. Means "the Way of the Sea" and refers to all or part of the main trade route from Mesopotamia to Egypt that ran through Israel.

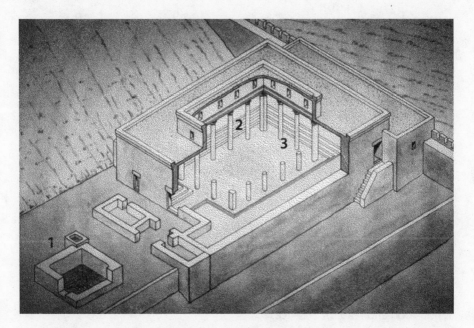

The Synagogue. This artist's interpretation of the synagogue at Gamla shows some of the features of a typical synagogue including (1) a mikveh, (2) stone benches for the important people, and (3) the columns to hold the roof. (*Leen Ritmeyer*)

when the Messiah came, He would control Har-Meggido once and for all, proving His power to the world.

Shmu'el arrived at the synagogue and found a place to sit among the other worshipers. The service started with the Sh'ma,[23] as had every religious gathering for hundreds of years, as the people recalled God's covenant and renewed their vows of obedience:

> *Hear, O Israel: The* LORD *our God, the* LORD *is one. Love the* LORD *your God with all your heart and with all your soul and with all your strength. These commandments that I give you today are to be upon your hearts. Impress them on your children. Talk about them when you sit at home and when you walk along the road, when you lie down and when you get up.* [24]

After the Sh'ma, seven members of the synagogue community read that Shabbat's allocated verses from the Torah and the Haphtarah.[25] Each reader, in

---

23. The opening prayer to all synagogue worship; it was also a statement of creed.
24. Deuteronomy 6:4–7
25. The books of the Prophets

turn, moved to Moshe's seat, where he waited for the attendant to hand him the proper scroll; then he stood to read.

That day, the elders had invited a visiting rabbi to read the final scripture. He was an itinerant teacher who had been gathering many disciples and followers in Galilee. He was also a native son of Natzeret. Some even said he had performed miracles and healings. Because of this and his growing reputation, the elders had asked the man to take the last reading from the Haphtarah and give the short sermon that always followed.

Waiting for the next reader to begin, Shmu'el looked around the synagogue. The people sat on mats on the stone floor. The elders filled the stone benches around the sides. The tall stone columns reached up to the open sky, the only roof the synagogue had ever known.

Finally, it was time for the last reading. The young teacher took his place, tassels hanging from the hem of his prayer shawl. The passage, according to the readings scheduled from the Torah and the Haphtarah for that Shabbat, was from the scroll of Yesha'yahu that spoke of the promised Messiah. The visiting rabbi stood and read the passage:

> The Spirit of the Sovereign LORD is on me,
>   because the LORD has anointed me to preach good news to the
>   poor.
> He has sent me to bind up the brokenhearted,
>   to proclaim freedom for the captives
>   and release from darkness for the prisoners,
> to proclaim the year of the LORD's favor. [26]

When he had finished, the teacher rolled up the scroll, handed it back to the attendant, and sat down.

His next words were the most startling—and the shortest sermon—Shmu'el had ever heard. "Today," he said, "this scripture has come true in me."

Then silence. Echoing silence.

Shock, anger, dismay, puzzlement—all these emotions swept through Shmu'el as he sat, stunned. *Where does this man get his authority?* he said to himself, then looked around, fearing he had said it aloud.

Most rabbis could teach only official doctrine, based on the authority of others. A few, however, carried the honor of s'mikhah[27] and could teach their

---

26. Isaiah 61:1–2a
27. Ordination or authority giving one the right to make legal judgments and new interpretations of the Law and the Prophets. It could be granted by a group of elders, at least one of whom had s'mikhah himself.

own interpretation of the Law. A rabbi who had been given such authority could say, "You have heard it said . . . but *I* say . . . "

When they heard the itinerant teacher's astonishing words, therefore, it was natural for those in the synagogue to wonder where this man had gotten his authority. And so young! He couldn't have been more than 30 years old. Shmu'el had never heard of anyone under the age of 40 having such authority to teach. Still, listening to the young rabbi answer questions in the dialogue that followed, Shmu'el was astounded at his wisdom and the graciousness with which he spoke.

Before the day was over, however, the elders of the synagogue were furious with the visiting teacher's pronouncements. It wasn't just his teaching or the fact that they couldn't prove his authority. He had let it be known that he would not localize his ministry in Natzeret and he refused to acknowledge that they were Messiah's exclusive community. He also brought his message to the Gentiles. What an insult this was to the Jews of Natzeret, who believed *they* were the shoot out of Yishai[28] from which the Messiah was to come!

Perhaps the final straw, though, was the man's refusal to perform miracles for them right there. Their initial positive reception turned to wrath, and they drove him out of town. Some went so far as to accuse him of blasphemy and would have thrown him over the cliff that looked out on the plain of Har-Meggido if it weren't for . . . well, Shmu'el wasn't quite sure why they hadn't.

Despite the way that day ended, Shmu'el couldn't erase the rabbi's strong but gentle voice and astonishing words from his mind.

Sometime later, rumors began circulating that this Rabbi Yeshua[29] was teaching strange interpretations of the Torah and the Haphtarah. Even the familiar parables he told took on new meaning, people said. Beyond that, he claimed his yoke was easy. Many students were leaving other rabbis for the easy yoke this teacher offered.

How can a rabbi's yoke be easy? Shmu'el wondered. The yoke of Torah was hard. It was *supposed* to be hard. Obedience did not come easily.

He wanted to test this Yeshua himself, as every teacher was tested from time to time. He wanted to ask him that very question: "How can the yoke of Torah be easy?"

Still, there had been something different, something unsettling about Yeshua, Shmu'el thought. Even more unsettling was the fact that he had felt the presence of God when this man taught.

---

28. Jesse
29. Jesus

Shmu'el's next memorable encounter with Yeshua was a year or two later in Yerushalayim. This time the man was teaching on the southern stairway of the Temple, outside the great Huldah Gates, where the people entered after cleansing themselves in the mikvoth[30] at the base of the steps. That evening, over dinner in the home of a friend in the upper city, Shmu'el and others argued vehemently about what the man had said, not unlike the rest of the city.

Yerushalayim was in an uproar that day. It was Passover week, and the crowds seemed greater than usual, the Roman presence more oppressive, and the Zealots crazier than ever. Shmu'el had planned to approach the teacher sometime during that week, hoping to question him. But before he could do that, the streets were filled with whispers about the man.

Apparently, a crowd of people had proclaimed him their political savior, welcoming him with palm branches and the great Hosannah chant for deliverance. Some were suggesting he was the Messiah. The Essenes were impressed that the first thing he did was to cleanse the Temple, challenging the Temple authority that the Essenes claimed was not legitimate anyway. Shmu'el had even met a woman from Beit-Anyah[31] who claimed that Yeshua had raised her brother from the dead.

Then, on the evening of Shabbat came the news that the Romans had crucified the man that very day. Some were even saying the Sanhedrin had helped arrange his execution because the man's followers were threatening to disturb its delicate balance of power with Rome.

After that, Shmu'el pushed Yeshua and his words to the back of his mind, trying to dismiss him as just another teacher. And yet, in the years following, he sometimes wondered, *If I had chosen to take his yoke, where would I be today? If we had all taken his yoke, would the Romans still be here?*

Nazareth, A.D. 68

Had he missed something that day? Shmu'el wondered now, looking around the destroyed synagogue. Was prophecy fulfilled here that day? Was God with them? Had he missed Him?

Shmu'el himself had been a rabbi for 40 years. How many parables had he himself taught? How many disciples had he nurtured? Education was never an academic affair, of course. Pointing out truth revealed in a bird, a flower, a lake, a funeral, a beggar, a leper, a tax collector—all those were particular events and

---

30. (sing. mikveh) Ritual baths
31. Bethany

opportunities to teach his students how to apply the Torah to specific situations—to show them how to live the way Jahweh wanted.

Still, his years of study had left him with as many questions as answers.

Shmu'el had heard that some of the Natzratim[32]—as the rabbi's students and followers were now called—still lived in Capernaum. Like him, they'd be old men now. But maybe he could track down at least one of them. Maybe he could ask the questions he hadn't asked all those years ago.

As he made his way through the rubble toward the front of the synagogue, he no longer heard the soldiers' voices. They must have moved on. Still, he hated to leave this place. Something told him he would never return.

He stepped outside onto the broad porch that ran across the front of the building. In the distance, he could see soldiers leading off several citizens in chains. He could hear their hammers pounding. The soldiers had already crucified the local leaders of the rebellion, but more executions were certain to follow.

Was this the way it all ended then? The Zealots said only power would bring in the kingdom. Well, they had brought in the kingdom all right—the kingdom of Caesar.

The old man fingered the tassels on the hem of his prayer shawl as his sandals carried him down the steps and toward the road to Capernaum.

Jesus' message and ministry were unique. He was the Son of God. His was the message of God. His was the ministry of death, resurrection, and redemption. Nothing quite like it had ever been seen or heard before; nothing like it has ever been seen or heard since.

Yet we miss a significant and crucial point if we fail to recognize that Jesus, in His earthly form and ministry, was a typical Jewish rabbi. He fit well into His world and culture. He had a great deal in common with the religious structures and the religious teaching that the Jewish people had been hearing for centuries.

Like other rabbis of His day, Jesus had disciples, He taught a yoke of Torah, and He communicated with people in a language and style they clearly understood. His examples and stories were familiar to His audience; only His interpretations were unique. His customs were similar, from the tassels on the edge of

---

32. (sing. Natzrati) Nazarenes

His robe to His faithful attendance at the feasts in Jerusalem, which He so frequently used as the basis for His teaching. Even His teaching methods were similar to those employed by the Pharisees, and the themes He stressed were common in certain religious movements of the times, such as the Essenes.

Like other rabbis, Jesus used images familiar to His audience—light and bread, sheep and water. And like other rabbis, He told parables, stories similar to those people had heard for centuries—but with a new twist. For example, in His culture people would expect a father to reject a son who left the Jewish faith and disgraced his family. Imagine the surprise of Jesus' listeners when He told the story of a prodigal son and at the end, the father went running to meet the son and cried, "My son was dead and now is alive!"

Through Jesus, God's great message of redemption, promised throughout the Old Testament, was communicated in a language and style meaningful to the people of that day. They understood what Jesus was saying and doing, whether they believed it or not.

But Jesus' ministry was not just about communication, knowledge, or understanding. Ultimately, His message had to make a difference in the lives of those who heard it.

"My yoke is easy," Jesus said.

First-century Jews knew all about the yoke of Torah: Didn't they have 613 commandments they must obey? And who knew how many interpretations of those commandments existed?

Sometimes Christians seem to think that when Jesus came, He threw off all the old biblical commandments and ushered in a new age of total freedom. Just love God and you'll be okay. But Jesus said:

> *Anyone who breaks one of the least of these commandments and teaches others to do the same will be called least in the kingdom of heaven, but whoever practices and teaches these commands will be called great in the kingdom of heaven. For I tell you that unless your righteousness surpasses that of the Pharisees and the teachers of the law, you will certainly not enter the kingdom of heaven.*

> *(Matthew 5:19–20)*

When Jesus said His yoke was easy, He meant it was easy to understand in contrast to the multitude of complex interpretations offered by other rabbis. His yoke was easy to understand, *but incredibly difficult to live.*

"Love God," said Jesus. "Love your neighbor."

That was easy to understand.

"Love your enemies. Be persecuted for righteousness. Care for the unclean, the leper, the weak, the sinner. Be honest. Don't be hypocrites. Be righteous!"

That was not easy to do.

"Take My yoke and learn from Me, for I am gentle and humble. Be My disciples," He said, "My talmidim. Learn by becoming like Me. Be like Me!"

> *A student is not above his teacher, but everyone who is fully*
> *trained will be like his teacher.*
>
> (Luke 6:40)

How rabbinical Jesus was! But gentleness and humility, not insensitive obedience, were at the heart of His yoke. "Do what the Pharisees tell you," He said, "not what they do."

Following Jesus isn't simply a matter of turning over our hearts and souls to Him; it means taking the yoke of His teaching and living it out day after day.

We all follow a "rabbi"—someone or something we strive to become like. We need to ask ourselves who our rabbi is.

If we're truly followers of Jesus, we'll do more than simply learn about Him, study what He taught, and memorize His words. Those are important in understanding who He was, how He lived, and what He would have us do. But as His disciples, we must be so totally committed to becoming like our Rabbi—in our words and actions; in our attitudes, thoughts, and feelings; in our concern and compassion for others; and in our desires—that others will want to become talmidim of Jesus as well.

Becoming like Jesus might seem too pious an endeavor for imperfect human beings to undertake, but it's really the ultimate in practicality. It all boils down to one question that needs to underlie every aspect of our lives: In this situation, with this person, what would Jesus do?

The goal of our lives must be to become like Jesus, our Rabbi.

Chapter 6

The Prayer Shawl

The LORD said to Moses, "Command the Israelites to send away from the camp anyone who has an infectious skin disease or a discharge of any kind, or who is ceremonially unclean because of a dead body. Send away male and female alike; send them outside the camp so they will not defile their camp, where I dwell among them." The Israelites did this; they sent them outside the camp. They did just as the LORD had instructed Moses.

(Numbers 5:1–4)

The LORD said to Moses, "Speak to the Israelites and say to them: 'Throughout the generations to come you are to make tassels on the corners of your garments, with a blue cord on each tassel. You will have these tassels to look at and so you will remember all the commands of the LORD, that you may obey them and not prostitute yourselves by going after the lusts of your own hearts and eyes. Then you will remember to obey all my commands and will be consecrated to your God. I am the LORD your God, who brought you out of Egypt to be your God. I am the LORD your God.'"

(Numbers 15:37–41)

This is what the LORD Almighty says: "In those days ten men from all languages and nations will take firm hold of one Jew by the hem of his robe and say, 'Let us go with you, because we have heard that God is with you.'"

(Zechariah 8:23)

But for you who revere my name, the sun of righteousness will rise with healing in its wings.

(Malachi 4:2a)

Just then a woman who had been subject to bleeding for twelve years came up behind him and touched the edge of his cloak. She said to herself, "If I only touch his cloak, I will be healed."

Jesus turned and saw her. "Take heart, daughter," he said, "your faith has healed you." And the woman was healed from that moment.

(Matthew 9:20–22;
Mark 5:25–34)

Everything they do is done for men to see: They make their phylacteries wide and the tassels on their garments long; they love the place of honor at banquets and the most important seats in the synagogues.

(Matthew 23:5–6)

And wherever he went—into villages, towns or countryside—they placed the sick in the marketplaces. They begged him to let them touch even the edge of his cloak, and all who touched him were healed.

(Mark 6:56)

Capernaum, A.D. 28

adassah[1] had tried everything—even the healing pool of Bethesda, outside the Temple in Yerushalayim.[2] The journey to the Holy City had been difficult, since her condition left her both weak and unclean. Her own people avoided her. Only a Gentile, a business friend of her father's, had been willing to help her. This man often traveled to Capernaum to buy millstones for his shop in Caesarea, and when her father told him of her desire to visit the healing pool in Yerushalayim, the merchant offered her a place in his caravan.

The Gentile's kindness had meant so much to her, though it could never dispel the cloud of loneliness that hovered over her. The long periods of hemorrhaging had begun when she was 14 and of marriageable age, so no one had wanted to marry her. And for 10 years now, because of her presence in their home, her family had had to go for ritual cleansing each time they wanted to enter the synagogue or the Temple. Ordinarily, such cleansing was necessary only after a death or a woman's monthly course, but her loved ones were subjected to this constant public disgrace. For this reason, no one wanted to come near her or risk the possibility of touching her.

Hadassah had never realized how important the touch of others was until she had been denied it. Truly she was outside the gates, outside the camp. She couldn't go into the synagogue or the Temple. She was impure.

Lepers had to shout "Unclean!" when anyone approached. She didn't have to do that, but in reality she was no different from them. Isolated. Cut off. Untouchable.

Even at Bethesda, surrounded by the ill and infirm, she had somehow felt inferior. Though many around her suffered terrible physical deformities, blindness, or lameness, such maladies didn't make them untouchable, except by the strictest Pharisees, who believed any illness meant a person was cursed of God. So she sat there bereft and alone amid the stately, carved columns and graceful

---

1. Esther
2. Jerusalem

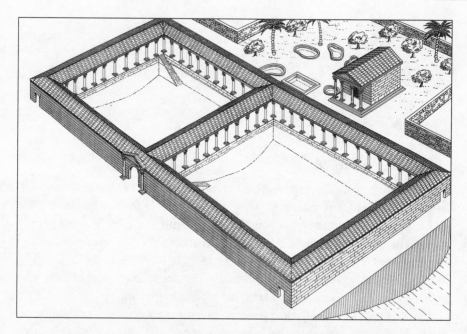

The Pool of Bethesda. Just north of the Temple Mount was this pool with five colonnades. Located near the Sheep Gate, it may have been used to prepare the animals for sacrifice in the Temple. Archaeologists found evidence of a small Roman temple to the god of healing nearby. (*Leen Ritmeyer*)

archways of the colonnades that surrounded the two rectangular, adjoining pools that were known as the pool of Bethesda.

The pools served a dual purpose, being used both as cisterns and as washing facilities for the nearby Temple. Since the pools collected runoff from the storm sewers of the city and were also used to wash the sacrificial sheep before they were taken through the Sheep Gate and into the Temple for sacrifice, the water was often dirty.

The sheep can go into the Temple, Hadassah thought, *but I, a daughter of Avraham,*[3] *can't.*

Even if she dared approach the steps of God's house, the Temple guards at the gates would inquire whether she was ritually clean and, when learning the truth, would immediately order her to leave. Through Moshe,[4] God had said, "Those who are unclean must live outside the camp where I dwell." Only if she could be healed could she be restored to the community.

The waters of Bethesda drew throngs of people every year. Many were so

---

3. Abraham
4. Moses

lame, crippled, or blind that they had to be carried into the pool. The area was particularly crowded when she was there, for it was the Feast of Pentecost, and the city was filled with pilgrims. The milling closeness of so many bodies, smelling of sweat and illness, made Hadassah dizzy and queasy, so she stayed back, sitting in the cool shade of the colonnade, leaning against a marble column for support.

Finally, when the crowd had diminished somewhat, she got up from the rose-colored paving stones and worked her way past several of the lame, who were lying on rugs and skins. She stepped onto the first step of the stairs that led down into the pool.

The water was murky and cold. Hadassah shivered as the wetness invaded her garments and slapped her warm skin. She stooped down until her shoulders were covered. She waited.

Nothing happened. She felt nothing except the chill of her clinging tunic.

She walked up the steps out of the pool and sank down on the warm stones. As she sat in the sun, waiting for her garments to dry, she watched men, women, and children entering the nearby temple of Aesculapius, the Greek and Roman god of medicine. Many Jews were offended that Herod had allowed a pagan temple to be built next to Jahweh's Temple. But people said it, too, had pools of healing water. For a moment, Hadassah was tempted.

No. She pushed the thought aside. Entering that pagan place would only carry her further from her people and her God.

Long ago, before she was even of marriageable age, she had decided that Jahweh was her salvation. No matter what happened, her only hope was faithfulness and obedience to her God. Still, when Hadassah returned home to Capernaum after her visit to the pool of Bethesda, she was disappointed and despairing.

Two cycles of the seasons had passed since then. Now it was 12 years since the onset of her disease. Twelve years of isolation and unbearable loneliness.

Recently, though, Hadassah had heard of a rabbi teaching in the area of Capernaum and Bethsaida. His interpretation of the Torah[5] was causing a stir. Some believed he might be the Messiah.

"He has healed many," people said. "Even a leper. Do we need more proof than this?"

One of those healed was from Capernaum, a man who had been paralyzed

---

5. The five books of Moses. The word *Torah* means "teachings," although it's often translated as "law."

for years. Hadassah knew the man. In fact, she had seen him in Yerushalayim near the pool when she was there two years before.

"How long have you been here?" she had asked him.

"Twenty-eight years," was his reply.

Now this same man could walk, people said.

Another person the rabbi had healed was the mother-in-law of one of the local fishermen. She had been bedridden, burning with fever. When the rabbi touched her hand, they said, the fever left.

He touched her, Hadassah thought. How she longed for someone to touch her with love and care, or even in sympathy. What had she done that she should be so shunned by her people? Perhaps by her God? Was He shunning her, too, through no fault of her own?

Yet this new rabbi, they said, touched those he healed.

Hadassah had heard her family talking about him. Her father said that their local rabbi had accused the man of blasphemy. But if God had sent him to do these wonderful things, showing His power as He had in the days of Moshe and Avraham, how could it be blasphemy?

She pulled open the wooden door to her room and looked out into the courtyard of the family insula.[6] Though she couldn't touch her nieces and nephews, couldn't smooth their dark, curly hair or kiss their soft cheeks, she could tell them stories. They loved her stories, and she cherished the times when they gathered near her and listened wide-eyed as she told them of her trip to Yerushalayim.

She described the dangerous journey on the steep and treacherous Yericho[7] Road where bandits often waylaid travelers and where one misstep could send you plunging from the narrow path to the wadi far below. She told them of the great Temple with its white marble and gold.

Little Yosi[8] had asked her, "What's it like to be in the Temple when the priest offers the sacrifice for our sins?"

She told them, calling it up from her distant memory of when her parents had taken her there as a child, barely suppressing her sadness at not being allowed there now.

Out of the corner of her eye, to her left, she glimpsed the mezuzah[9] mounted

---

6. (pl. insulae) A family household arrangement common in Capernaum and Korazin, where many rooms—residences for various family members—were built around a central courtyard.

7. Jericho

8. Nickname for Joseph

9. A hollowed-out tree branch mounted on the doorpost of a house to hold tiny, rolled parchments of Scripture. Today they're more elaborately designed and fashioned from ceramic, brass, or wood.

A Mezuzah. To fulfill God's command to put His words "on the doorframes of your houses and your gates," Jewish people fix small containers to their doorposts that contain the passage from Deuteronomy 4:6–9. (*Eyal Bartov*)

on the stone doorpost of her room. *Do this so you will remember,* God had commanded their people hundreds of years ago. Now this was her reminder to be faithful, to make God's Word part of her life, every time she passed through the doorway.

The hollowed-out tree branch, not much longer than her finger, contained tiny, rolled parchments bearing verses from the Torah:

> *Hear, O Israel: The LORD our God, the LORD is one. Love the LORD your God with all your heart and with all your soul and with all your strength. These commandments that I give you today are*

*to be upon your hearts. . . . Write them on the doorframes of your
houses and on your gates.*[10]

Each time Hadassah crossed the threshold, she rubbed the wood of the mezuzah, once rough and knobby, now worn smooth from her touch. *So you will remember.*

Through the doorway, a sliver of Gennesaret[11] glimmered in the distance. Oh, to be strong enough to walk along the blue sea again. To smell the water. To feel the warmth of the sun on her shoulders and pick the scarlet poppies. To grind her own flour and make her own cloth. Oh, to be clean again. To be part of the community. To be touched.

"Y̓ou should have been out fishing with us yesterday," said Kefa.[12] "You would have had enough adventure to last you at least a few months."

"Did you get caught in that storm?" Gid'on[13] asked.

"We sure did. The wind came up from the east, and the waves kicked up so fast we were almost swamped—with a big catch. Took us forever to get back to shore. Then it stopped as suddenly as it started—I've never seen anything like it. It was as if a giant hand smoothed the waves. Still, we blew out a sail, and I've spent all morning mending it."

Whenever Gid'on heard about his friend's narrow escapes on the water, he was thankful for his own mundane trade. Making millstones might not be exciting, but it was safe. Besides, he was proud to have a part in producing the famous Capernaum millstones. People came from as far south as Beersheba and as far north as Caesarea Philippi to buy them.

Like Gid'on, most Jews stayed close to the shoreline and wouldn't think of sailing across to the other side. Their ancestors had often sung of their intense fear of water, even the water that raced down the wadis after rain.

> *Save me, O God,*
> > *for the waters have come up to my neck.*
> *I sink in the miry depths,*
> > *where there is no foothold.*
> *I have come into the deep waters;*
> > *the floods engulf me.*[14]

---

10. Deuteronomy 6:4–6,9
11. The Sea of Galilee; also known as the Sea of Tiberias after Herod Antipas's capital city, Tiberias, which he named for his friend the Roman emperor Tiberius.
12. Peter
13. Gideon
14. Psalm 69:1–2

A Millstone. This flour mill, made of basalt, was found in Capernaum. The hard volcanic rock of the area made excellent material for millstones like this one. Handles on each side were used to turn the stone, which fit over a cone. Grain was poured into the top, and flour sifted out of the bottom. (*Ray Vander Laan*)

The depths of the sea had always been a fearful thing to the Jews. They were desert people. Besides, the Canaanites who had ruled this land before them had worshiped Baal, the god of storms and the sea. Perhaps that was why many thought demons lived beneath the water.

Gid'on had no trouble believing that about this abyss. Though on the surface it looked beautiful and calm, he shivered at the thought of what might lurk in the dark depths.

Today, though, the lake was misty, the far shore disappearing in clouds and light rain. You wouldn't get him out on that water for all the fish in Gennesaret. Storms blew up too quickly. Without warning. Plenty of lives had been lost there.

"I'll stay safely on dry land, thank you very much," Gid'on said to Kefa.

"I hear you're planning to study with a rabbi," said Kefa, rolling his eyes and changing the subject. "Do you know who yet?"

"No," said Gid'on. "But I'm thinking seriously about following Yeshua."[15] The new teacher's use of Torah was refreshingly different. Even the familiar teaching parables took on new life when he interpreted them or applied them. "I think I would like to become a rabbi myself," Gid'on said.

"That will take years," said Kefa. "I never imagined you becoming a talmid."[16]

"Neither did I," Gid'on said, "until I met Yeshua."

Though he had been studying Torah for several months now, he still remembered a time when he used to get tired of Galilee and its religion-obsessed inhabitants. If it wasn't the Pharisees arguing over interpretations of the oral law, it was the Zealots with their dreams of revolution. For a brief time, he had even considered leaving the area. One of his friends from Beth Midrash[17] had done that when he was 16.

"I'm going to 'the other side'[18] and enjoy life!" his friend had said, and had demanded his share of the family inheritance before he left. A year later he was back, destitute and starving and begging to return to his father's household, if only as a servant. His father had slammed the door in his face. The townspeople had consoled the father and commended him for his just treatment of the boy.

I wonder whatever became of him, Gid'on thought. *I could never risk losing my family and community the way he did.*

Gid'on would rather die than face his father's displeasure or be cut off from his family forever. His sister's life was hard enough. Though Hadassah was still part of their insula community, her illness kept her apart. He saw the sorrow in her eyes and the burden of her isolation in the slump of her shoulders.

But his decision had done more than please his father. Until he had begun his serious study of Torah, he hadn't realized how discipleship could change his life.

He fingered the tzitziyot[19] sewn to the hem of his outer garment as he paced the stone courtyard of his family's insula. As commanded by Jahweh in the book of Numbers, each tassel had eight threads. "One of the threads used to be purple," their local rabbi had taught them in Beth Midrash. That meant costly

---

15. Jesus
16. (pl. talmidim) A disciple or student of a rabbi whose desire was not only to know what his teacher knew but also to become like him.
17. A secondary synagogue school at which Jewish boys who had celebrated their bar mitzvahs (at 12 or 13; the term *bar mitzvah* wasn't used in Jesus' time) could study Torah and the oral traditions of their faith.
18. Also known as the Decapolis; the area on the eastern side of the Sea of Galilee and the Jordan River that included a confederation of self-ruled Hellenistic cities.
19. (sing. tzitzit) Tassels, as on a prayer shawl

The Prayer Shawl. In Jesus' time, this outer garment had tassels on the corners in obedience to God's command. Today, religious Jews like this man at the Western Wall of the Temple Mount in Jerusalem use an outer shawl, called a prayer shawl, on special days. Note the tassel hanging from the edge of the shawl. (*Leon Bangma*)

purple dye, the color of royalty, to remind them that they were a kingdom of priests, a royal nation.

"But since purple is also a royal color for the Romans, we no longer wear it," said the rabbi.

The tassels themselves were also a mark of royalty. Kings and priests wore them as a sign of their office, said the rabbi. Daveed[20] had cut off King Saul's tassels at the cave at En Gedi, stripping him of the symbol of his royal office.

---

20. David

One . . . two . . . three . . . four . . . five. Gid'on counted the knots. The rabbis taught that each tzitzit had five knots, reminders of God's covenant and laws in the five books of Moshe, and the four spaces between the knots represented the name of God with its four letters—the name no one dared speak except the high priest on Yom Kippur, the day of atonement. And the way the knots were wrapped and tied was a reminder of the Sh'ma[21]: "Hear, O Israel: The LORD our God . . . the LORD is one."

Gid'on was proud of his tassels. They set him apart as a member of God's chosen people. And he was proud that he could recite all 613 commandments in the Torah—so many to remember, so many to obey.

Even the prophet Z'karyah[22] had spoken of the significance of these tassels and the power of faithfulness. People would reach out and grab the tassels of a person they knew was faithful, said the prophet, acknowledging that God was with him.

> *This is what the LORD Almighty says: "In those days ten men from all languages and nations will take firm hold of one Jew by the hem [tassels] of his robe and say, 'Let us go with you, because we have heard that God is with you.'"*[23]

"Messiah will have healing in the tassels of his robe," said the rabbi at their synagogue. "That was what Malachi the prophet meant when he said the Messiah will have healing in his wings." It was the local rabbi's opinion that the wings were the edges of the Messiah's cloak.

"When Messiah comes, he won't need to show off his tassels," said others. "His faithfulness to the Almighty will speak for itself."

"But that is exactly why Messiah will have miraculous power in his tassels," said the rabbi. "His tassels will have healing power and power of forgiveness because he will keep all of the Law perfectly."

Most men in Gid'on's community wore tassels on their outer garments, and some sewed them on the outer robes they wore for their public or daily prayers. They didn't do this because there was merit in wearing tzitziyot, but because God had commanded it as a way of reminding them of Him.

Some men, however, wore extra-long tassels; they believed that showed how faithful they were. Seeing the lengths some went to, Gid'on thought perhaps

---

21. The opening prayer to all synagogue worship; it was also a statement of creed.
22. Zechariah
23. Zechariah 8:23

they wanted others to wonder if they were the Messiah. The rabbi had criticized these Pharisees because they were giving the many faithful Pharisees of Galilee a bad name.

Hadassah had heard more rumors about the new teacher, Yeshua. He was coming back to Capernaum! Her family had talked of nothing else last night as they gathered in the courtyard after the evening meal. Her brother Gid'on had even spoken of possibly becoming one of his talmidim.

If only I could get near enough to see this teacher, to hear him, she thought. *If only I could get near enough to touch him, I might find the healing others have found.*

Then this morning, about midmorning, she'd heard excited voices in the courtyard. "Yeshua is here. He's in the town square."

Hadassah went to the doorway and looked out. Her father, two of her uncles, Gid'on, and one of her sisters were already preparing to leave. She stroked the mezuzah. *Remember. Remember. Be faithful.*

What if she followed her family, keeping her distance?

Because this Yeshua often taught outdoors, like the other rabbis, she could hear him. If he had stayed within the synagogue, she would have been forbidden. But what if she hid behind one of the olive trees that lined the town square? She could watch and listen to his words, and no one would be offended or disturbed by her presence.

Could this rabbi be Messiah, as some are saying? Hadassah wondered. Many said that he healed; some vowed that he had raised people from the dead, just as the prophets had predicted. Other prophets of God had done both, of course. But Yeshua's life—that's what was different, people said.

His interpretations of the Law were controversial at times, but she had heard no one accuse him of breaking Torah. And if he was perfectly faithful to the Torah, then he must be Messiah. And if he was Messiah, then he was able to heal.

Should she or shouldn't she? Suddenly the thought struck her: *His tassels! Messiah will have healing in the tassels at the hem of his garment.*

But how could she get close enough to touch him? If she tried to mingle with the crowd, they would send her away, afraid of her uncleanness. And if by chance she could get close enough, would he do the same?

No. Messiah would never send her away.

Hadassah went to the cupboard and took down her haluk[24] and her veil.

---

24. Outer garment

Perhaps if she wrapped her cloak closely about her and kept her face covered with her veil, they wouldn't recognize her.

She touched the mezuzah one more time and left the house.

Hundreds of years before Jesus was born, the prophet Malachi had foretold the Messiah who would come "with healing in his wings." To some, that meant He had healing "in the edges of his clothing." And the prophet Zechariah had predicted that people from every nation would want to clutch the hem or the tassel of the Messiah's garment because they would recognize that God was with Him.

Every faithful male Jew wore tassels on the hem of his garment, just as God, in the Old Testament, had commanded. "Do this to remember Me," God said. To them, as the Lord's Supper is for us, the tassels were a reminder of what God had done and of the importance of obedience.

Some Jews believed, however, that the Messiah's tassels would somehow have special significance or meaning, representing both His total commitment to obedience of God's law and His unique powers of forgiveness and healing. So when the woman who had had "an issue of blood" for 12 years grabbed "the edge of his cloak," she very likely grabbed His tassels.

This wasn't simply a desperate plea for healing. It wasn't just an "I'll try anything" last resort. This was her affirmation that she recognized the messianic character of Jesus and His work. She believed He was the Messiah. Because she believed that—because of her great faith—the power of Jesus flowed through her. It healed her body, and it restored her to the community from which she had been separated for so long.

And the magic wasn't only in Jesus' touch; it was in His righteousness. People recognized Him as the Messiah because of His holiness. Moses had healed. Elijah had raised the dead. So those acts, miraculous as they were, were not what set Jesus apart. Those would have made Him one of the great prophets. What set Him apart was His perfect obedience to the Father. And, He said, all who obey Him would do *even greater* works!

We, too, can work to restore others to the community of faith. Our acceptance of, our commitment to, and our testimony of the reality of Jesus being not only *the* Messiah but also *our* Messiah opens us to become channels of God's healing and renewing power, whether for our own physical, emotional, and spiritual brokenness or for the needs of others.

Throughout the Bible, we see the power of God flowing through people who submitted themselves totally to Him. Think of Abraham leading his beloved son up that mountain of sacrifice. Think of David, who submitted to God even when guilty of great sin. Think of Moses, Elijah, Rahab, and Daniel. The list goes on and on.

When we come to that kind of submission to Jesus as our Messiah and Lord, we can be powerful channels of God's grace. To do that, we must go through the same process the woman of faith went through as she reached for His tassels. First we experience the Messiah's healing and restoration, and then we become channels of the same to others.

As the perfectly obedient Son of God who fulfilled the Law in every part, Jesus became the ultimate channel of His Father's great power. This, then, becomes our model.

It's true that forgiveness is a gift from God, that we never attain perfection in this life, and that the power of the Spirit is absolutely necessary to carry out God's will. But God has always honored and used faithful obedience, and He continues to do so today. His power surges most effectively through obedient people.

"If you remember . . . if you obey," God says, "My power will flow through you."

Chapter 7

The Theater

> Be careful not to do your "acts of righteousness" before men, to
> be seen by them. . . . So when you give to the needy, do not
> announce it with trumpets, as the hypocrites do in the synagogues
> and on the streets, to be honored by men. I tell you the truth, they
> have received their reward in full.
>
> (Matthew 6:1–2)

> When you fast, do not look somber as the hypocrites do, for
> they disfigure their faces to show men they are fasting. I tell you the
> truth, they have received their reward in full.
>
> (Matthew 6:16)

Sepphoris, about A.D. 10

Lost shall be the name on the land,
    all gone, perished.
Troy, city of sorrow, is there no longer. . . .
    Mourn for the ruined city, then go away
to the ships of the Achaeans. [1]

he chorus of voices echoed, then faded. The actors departed. High in the empty theater, 11-year-old Natan'el[2] watched in awe and wonder, the dramatic words ringing in his ears. *What will happen next?* he wondered.

He looked down across the huge semicircular seating area facing the stage, squinting against the glare of the noonday sun on the white limestone. Now that he wasn't concentrating on the actors rehearsing the play, he almost became dizzy from the brightness and the height. Lost in the words and actions on the stage below, he had unconsciously sat down in the top tier of the theater.

Now several actors drifted out between the tall marble columns lining the back of the stage. Although they were no longer speaking their lines, the acoustics were so good that Natan'el could almost hear their conversation, even though they were talking in ordinary tones.

The man who seemed to be in charge, ordering the actors and everyone else about, walked down the steps from the stage and stepped onto the open pavement between the stage and the seating area. The workmen had finished setting the tiles there yesterday, and the pavement was now one huge, multicolored mosaic, picturing images of the Greek gods and goddesses. The man seemed oblivious to the beauty beneath his feet. He watched the actors for a while, then turned and looked up at the tiers of carved benches of white limestone, iridescent in the sunlight.

---

1. Euripides, "Trojan Women," in *Euripides III*, ed. by David Grene and Richmond Lattimore, trans. by Richmond Lattimore (Chicago: University of Chicago Press, 1958), p. 174.
2. Nathanael

The Theater. This Roman theater was found in Beth Shean (Scythopolis), one of the cities of the Decapolis. It had seating for 7,000 spectators. Only the lower of three tiers of seats remains, though the stone base for the second tier can still be seen. (*Ray Vander Laan*)

Is the man imagining what the place will look like with an audience? Natan'el wondered. Row upon row rose against the blue sky to seat more than 4,000 people. That was the theater's capacity, his father said.

Four thousand! Natan'el couldn't imagine that many people going to the theater. For his people, the Jews, such wicked places were off-limits. It was against Jewish law to paint or portray any human form, and the theater, when completed, would be decorated with nude statues. Here they would celebrate their pagan religious festivals and feasts.

Still, Natan'el was fascinated by the actors. *Hypocrites* was their name in Greek, he had been told. They pretended to be something they weren't.

The name fits, Natan'el thought.

In a moment, these men could be transformed. They could even become women, waving their arms and robes! They disguised their true selves beneath costumes and paint. Even their emotions weren't real. They showed fear or hatred, happiness or sadness, anger or love, by painting their faces black or white. Natan'el had seen them.

Below the stage were dozens of cubicles where the actors dressed and waited for their entrances. Yesterday he had snuck down the steps hidden at the side of the stage behind a column and wandered about below. He had watched the men paint their faces and tried to listen as they talked and gulped wine from drinking cups shaped like winged creatures. Their Greek accent made their Aramaic difficult to understand at times, and his Greek wasn't good enough for him to follow much when they lapsed into their own tongue. So some of their conversation didn't make sense to him, and some seemed crude or obscene. But one exchange that he caught had intrigued him.

"Why did King Herod Antipas choose this particular play for our first performance here?" one of the actors had asked another.

"Yes," agreed a third. "Why not *The Bacchae* or *Electra?*" he said, naming two other plays by the same famous Greek playwright, Euripides.

"Perhaps Herod is trying to make a point," said a man whose features had been painted to portray a woman in mourning. "After all, it shows what happens to someone who resists those in power!"

"I really don't care," one said with a laugh, "as long as they applaud. I just live for the applause anyway."

The actors ignored Natan'el, but a workman who was putting the finishing touches on some of the plastered hallway walls finally chased him away.

Natan'el wanted to ask his father if he knew what the actors meant, but he was afraid to tell him he had been beneath the stage, eavesdropping. Bad enough that he had confessed to listening to the actors rehearse. His father hadn't scolded him for watching the play, but he had reprimanded him for neglecting his work.

I wonder if the actors could tell some of the stories from the Torah,[3] Natan'el wondered. If they could act out this story about this place called Troy, why couldn't they act out some of the great dramatic stories of Avraham[4] and Moshe[5]? What would happen if you put the story of the Torah into a play—

"Natan'el, where are you?" his father's shout interrupted.

The boy jumped up, grabbed his wooden mallet from the bench, and hurried through the elegant arched passageway that led to the gallery behind the upper level of seats where he and his father had been working for several days.

"I'm sorry, Father," Natan'el said. "I was watching the actors again. It's so interesting, and I wanted to see how the story ended."

---

3. The five books of Moses. The word *Torah* means "teachings," although it's often translated as "law."
4. Abraham
5. Moses

"Forget about that. Stop wasting time," his father scolded. "Herod's foreman will be along any minute now to check our work."

Natan'el knew his father wasn't exaggerating just to make him work harder. The king's foreman stopped by every day. Herod was anxious for the theater to be finished and demanded constant updates on their progress. The foreman said the king had even set the day for the opening celebration. All the workmen and artisans had to be done by then. The play the actors were rehearsing now would be performed for the opening of the theater in this newly constructed city of Sepphoris.

Today, Natan'el and his father were setting the final course of stone around the back of the theater.

Natan'el was surprised that his father wasn't angry at him for listening to the actors. But, then, it was rather astounding that he and his father were working here at all. His father and their rabbi at the synagogue in Natzeret[6] had argued about the matter. The rabbi said they shouldn't be working on any building in this city, and especially not the theater.

"Hypocrites!" said the rabbi. Natan'el was surprised he would even use the Greek word. "Pretending to be what they aren't. Don't you know that a man who follows the Torah should never darken the entrance of a theater, not even with his shadow?"

Hadn't God destroyed their first Temple, built by King Daveed's[7] son, because of the people's idolatry and pagan sexual practices—the very things being portrayed in these plays and acted out on these stages by the Greeks and the Romans? How could God be with people who practiced such things?

"The immorality of their plays. The images carved into their theaters and displayed by the actors. Acting out the stories of false gods and goddesses. The obscenity of their sexual practices and their drunken orgies. Are these not horrible enough?" said the rabbi.

"The theater isn't finished yet," replied Natan'el's father, "but I've seen and heard no orgies. And it is honest labor. Every tekton[8] in Natzeret is employed there," he added. "And who else is hiring workmen besides Herod?"

For many years, Sepphoris had been the largest city in Galilee, as well as its capital. During Herod the Great's reign, the city had been an important military post, with many armaments and provisions stored there. After the king's death, however, sensing the confusion and weakness in the government caused by

---

6. Nazareth
7. David
8. A stonemason or builder; sometimes translated as "carpenter."

disputes over who would inherit the throne, Jewish revolutionaries had taken charge. They didn't want another Herod. So they had stolen the weapons and made the city the headquarters of their rebellion.

After Antipas's right to rule had been established by the emperor in Rome, the Roman legion, under the command of Varis, had brutally attacked the Jews at Sepphoris. The Romans burned the city and killed the citizens or sold them into slavery.

Then Antipas had begun rebuilding Sepphoris. Although the city was still predominantly Jewish, it was heavily influenced by Greek and Roman culture. Many of its citizens, believing it was futile to resist Rome, had decided it was more sensible to live in peaceful coexistence. "Sepphoris will be a jewel of a city," they proclaimed, "the jewel of Galilee."

With its colonnaded streets paved with mosaic tiles or herringbone-patterned stones, rows of shops, and beautiful theater, Sepphoris now bore no resemblance to the city that had been destroyed just a few years before. For this reason, many of the religious Jews in Galilee, including Natan'el's rabbi in Natzeret, wanted nothing to do with Herod's "ornament of Galilee."

Still, Natan'el's father had not been dissuaded. Herod's massive building program drew the entire labor force from the surrounding countryside. The city had running water, brought from mountain springs by an aqueduct to an enormous cistern, where it was stored and then carried to the city by a water wheel. How many workmen had it taken just to build those two things?

Each day, Natan'el and his father, along with many other workers, walked almost three miles from their small town of Natzeret, with its 150 people, to this city of 35,000, the largest in Galilee.

The people of Natzeret had decided that the Messiah was to come from their town. Yet when he compared the two cities, Natan'el sometimes wondered why Messiah would come from a little place like Natzeret when Sepphoris was so grand.

Just then the high, brassy notes of a trumpet echoed against the stones. Drawn by the sound, Natan'el wandered back inside the theater. What was happening now? He had watched the rehearsals enough to know that the entrance of each of the main actors was announced by the sound of the trumpet.

"Natan'el! Get back to work!" his father called.

The boy returned and resumed setting stones.

A fternoon shadows were long by the time Natan'el and his father started south along the paved Roman road that ran between Sepphoris and Natzeret. Natan'el liked to count the carved stone pillars that marked each mile. Each mile marker was inscribed with the distance and the name of the emperor, Augustus. Roman law said that a Roman soldier could make any passerby carry his load of personal goods and equipment for one of those miles. Natan'el had never had that happen, but some of his friends had. Just one more reason, they said, to hate the Romans, always imposing their heavy hand.

He hurried along beside his father and the other workers. On both sides of the road, the hillsides were heavily terraced to conserve the soil and moisture for farming. The silvery green leaves of the olive trees whispered in the evening breeze.

Somewhere it had been raining. Natan'el could see the bow in the sky. It looked as if it might reach all the way down to Gennesaret.[9] He had been there only once, the longest journey his father had ever taken him on. Next year, however, he would travel all the way to Yerushalayim[10] to make his first Passover.

Thinking of that, he began to recite the Torah to himself. To become an adult and pray in the synagogue, he had to have the entire five books of Moshe memorized.

Looking back at Sepphoris, perched like a great white bird on its hilltop, Natan'el's curiosity overcame his fear of reprimand. He told his father about the conversation he had overheard beneath the stage. "Why would Herod want to have a play about what happens to enemies?" Natan'el asked.

"Perhaps as a warning for the future," said his father. "Sepphoris has a bloody history. Many of our people were crucified there a few years ago because they cooperated with those who revolted against Rome after Herod the Great's death. Their rebellion caused its destruction—the reason it is being rebuilt today."

"Father, the city is so much bigger and more beautiful than Natzeret," said Natan'el. "Do you think the Messiah might come there instead of to our town?"

"Never, my son!" replied his father. "We of Natzeret belong to the family of Yishai,[11] Daveed's father. The name of our town was chosen because Natzeret means 'a shoot' or 'a branch.' Messiah will be the shoot from Yishai's family—our family."

After they had walked a bit farther, Natan'el's father called out to a man walking ahead of them, another stonemason from Natzeret.

"Yosef,[12] I see your son is not with you today. Will he soon be learning our trade?"

---

9. The Sea of Galilee; also known as the Sea of Tiberias after Herod Antipas's capital city, Tiberias, which he named for his friend the Roman emperor Tiberius.
10. Jerusalem
11. Jesse
12. Joseph

"He's already accomplished at carving stone," Yosef said. "But he loves to study with the rabbi. He'll soon be making his first Passover, so I do without him whenever I can."

Natan'el knew Yosef's son well. A year or two older than Natan'el, he was a bright, honest boy who loved to be outdoors with the birds and animals as much as he seemed to love learning the Torah. Everyone liked him, although Natan'el always thought there was something that set him apart from the other boys. Probably he would be a rabbi someday—a very wise one.

Natan'el kicked at the thought as he rolled a stone ahead of him with his sandals, batting it back and forth, trying to keep it from losing its way in the grassy verge. He loved Adonai,[13] but he wouldn't want to be cooped up in the synagogue school all day. He enjoyed working with his hands and with his father, and he loved all the exciting things he saw each day in Sepphoris. His father said that Herod's foreman had told him they would soon begin to build another great city. This one was to be called Tiberias, and it would sit beside Gennesaret. His father said they would probably go there to work when they were finished at Sepphoris.

Natan'el could hardly wait. He wondered if there would be a theater there, too.

Did Jesus attend the theater in Sepphoris, only a few miles from His home in Nazareth? Probably not. But He certainly had to be aware of its existence and influence. In fact, it's possible that Jesus and His father, Joseph, helped in the rebuilding of Sepphoris, because Herod Antipas's building programs were so massive that he must have employed thousands of craftsmen and workers from the surrounding areas.

Although Jesus lived in a world of religious peasants in bustling agricultural villages along the shoreline of the Sea of Galilee and in the surrounding hills, He also lived in a world that glittered with the sophisticated pagan culture of the Greeks and Romans. Consequently, He often alluded to aspects of that world to illustrate His messages. He is the only New Testament writer or speaker who referred to the theater and actors—their painted faces, the trumpets announcing their entrances, and their love of applause. He used these colorful images to describe those whose faith is mere performance rather than heartfelt.

---

13. God

In His desire to communicate in a language the people of His world could understand, Jesus commonly referred to aspects of culture that would clearly convey His unique message of salvation and righteousness. He did not develop some arcane religious vocabulary, nor did He speak solely in the understandable but confined language of the rabbi. He commanded the language of the fisher- man, the housewife, the businessman, the tax collector, the farmer, the vineyard owner, the olive and wine presser, the shepherd, the soldier, the king—and the pagan. Without ever participating in or accepting their values and beliefs, Jesus used a language that pagans related to and understood.

The religious Jewish community of that time isolated itself from the larger Hellenistic and Romanized culture, with its violence, brutality, pagan values, open obscenities, and perverted sexuality. To religious Jews, all of this was evil and violently anti-God, and the rabbis and other religious authorities demanded complete separation from that pagan world by those who would follow the God of Abraham, Isaac, and Jacob.

Yet Jesus displayed a remarkable ability, while always maintaining His commitment to God's ways and values, to communicate with the people of that world, the people who participated in the paganism of their culture. He could dispute the finer points of theology with the Pharisees, He could touch the hearts and minds of peasants and fishermen with His stories, and He could speak the language of the wealthy aristocracy of His day.

Certainly, separation from the pagan world is important when we're speaking about our own life and behavior. But when we're talking about reaching our culture, we need to think in different terms. God's message is not simply for those who are like us, who are committed to the same morality, the same lifestyle, the same traditions. His message is for everyone, and it's our responsi- bility as Christians to communicate it to the sophisticated, cultured, and very pagan world in which we live.

Like Jesus, we must communicate God's message to the people we encounter every day. One person might thrill to the medium of music; another is online in cyberspace. One person enjoys reading newsmagazines; another watches CNN. One person appreciates great paintings and attends the symphony; another tunes in to MTV and video games. All of them need to hear about Jesus.

Though we must never compromise our values and beliefs to fit into the world around us, we need to understand that world—its language, technologies, methods of communication, and values—if we're to deliver effectively God's message of salvation by faith in Jesus Christ.

Chapter 8

The Zealot

You have heard that it was said, "Love your neighbor and hate your enemy." But I tell you: Love your enemies and pray for those who persecute you, that you may be sons of your Father in heaven.
(Matthew 5:43–45a)

No one can serve two masters. Either he will hate the one and love the other, or he will be devoted to the one and despise the other.
(Matthew 6:24)

These are the names of the twelve apostles: first, Simon (who is called Peter) and his brother Andrew . . . Simon the Zealot and Judas Iscariot, who betrayed him.
(Matthew 10:2,4)

Then he said to them, "Give to Caesar what is Caesar's, and to God what is God's."
(Matthew 22:21b)

After him, Judas the Galilean appeared in the days of the census and led a band of people in revolt. He too was killed, and all his followers were scattered.
(Acts 5:37)

Gamla, A.D. 28

Eagles glided above the cliffs as El'azar[1] made his way along the steep hillside. Usually sure-footed, in his haste he tripped over the rocks in the stony path that snaked downward toward the sea. Stopping to gain his footing and catch his breath, he looked down the long valley to Gennesaret,[2] its waters silver in the sunlight.

Blackbirds, swooping high above, called to him. He watched them longingly. Oh, to be that free. Those who hoped in the Almighty would soar on wings like eagles, the prophet had said. Would El'azar's land, his people, ever be that free?

Here on the lush, green fields of the heights, bright with spring flowers, he could look out across the silvery, oval sea, surrounded by foothills and mountains. On its western shore sprawled the town of Tiberias. The people there supported Herod Antipas, traitors to the Jewish cause. Built more than 10 years ago by Antipas and named for the emperor of the despised invaders, the city's gold-roofed palace glittered in the sun. A few miles north of that was El'azar's destination.

He turned his eyes to the south, where another high hill was crowned by the city of Hippos, defended by the Roman legions. He couldn't see the walled city through the early-morning haze, but he knew it was there. Sometimes he imagined his enemies gazing back at him. He fingered the knife at his belt. *Despicable Romans,* he thought. He despised their arrogance as much as he hated their pagan practices and beliefs—their gods and goddesses and their debauchery.

El'azar shook his head. He had no time to dwell on such things now. He still had a six-mile journey ahead of him, down to the sea and then around the north shore to the town of Capernaum in Galilee, where he was to meet with Shim'on.[3]

---

1. Eleazar
2. The Sea of Galilee; also known as the Sea of Tiberias after Herod Antipas's capital city, Tiberias, which he named for his friend the Roman emperor Tiberius.
3. Simon

The Home of the Zealots. The ruins of Gamla (meaning "camel" in Aramaic) are still standing on the steep hillside just east of the Sea of Galilee (upper right). The defensive tower (upper right), the gate, the synagogue, and the breach made by the Romans when they destroyed the city (lower left) can still be seen. (*Ray Vander Laan*)

Galilee. The land of the 12, some called it—after the 12 faithful tribes of Israel. Land of the religious faithful. Home of the Pharisees, with a synagogue in every town. Their answer to every issue was always the same: "Obey the Torah.[4] If we obey, God will protect us."

And what had it gotten them? Enslaved to Rome just like everyone else! Obedience was fine, but it hadn't driven out the Romans or brought his people political freedom. Herod and Pilate still ruled the land. *Our land!* El'azar thought savagely. *Land given to us by the Almighty. Promised to us. Won for us by our ancestors, by Y'hoshua,[5] Saul, and Daveed.[6]*

As El'azar descended the winding path that took him through the terraced olive groves and vineyards hugging the hillside above the shore, he wondered about the urgency of his cousin's message, delivered by one of their courier-

---

4. The five books of Moses. The word *Torah* means "teachings," although it's often translated as "law."
5. Joshua
6. David

spies. "Come as quickly as possible. Exciting news!" Knowing Shim'on, "exciting" meant something to do with their movement.

Before El'azar set his sandals on the path that would lead him around the northern end of the sea, he looked back toward the heights. At the end of the long valley, the high plateau rose misty green, the city of Gamla barely visible on its crown. His family and their compatriots had chosen this place years before because of its invincible position. Sloping sharply downward on three sides, the rocky plateau was linked to the higher hill beyond by a narrow ridge, leaving only one major defense point. Gamla, with its houses and synagogue, now terraced down its sides in such a way that his mother claimed that everyone's roof was someone else's front yard.

"No one will ever take us off our mountain," his fiercely independent father often bragged, pointing to their stone walls and high watchtower. "Like our Maccabean ancestors, we bow our knee to no one but God. On Hanukkah,[7] we wave the palm branches high to honor their heroism, their bold and brave defiance of the Romans." As he said it, he would raise his fist high in the air, clutching an invisible branch.

"The Almighty supports our cause," his father said. "We're the faithful remnant. The holy war was His idea in the first place. We have been the only ones obedient and faithful to drive the pagans out of our land."

Serve no one but Jahweh. Pay taxes only to Jahweh and His Temple. Slavery to the Roman is worse than death. El'azar had had that credo pounded into him.

hen he arrived at the bustling seaside town of Capernaum, famous for its production of millstones and olive presses, El'azar stopped to ask a fellow Zealot about his cousin's whereabouts and learned he was staying with two brothers. The man directed him to a large insula[8] close to the shore.

El'azar spotted Shim'on sitting with a group of men under a grove of olive trees near the house. They were talking and gesturing excitedly as he approached, but Shim'on noticed him immediately and beckoned for him to join them.

"El'azar, I'm glad you came so promptly."

"How could I ignore such an urgent message? I thought perhaps you'd discovered the lost ark."

---

7. Also known as the Feast of Dedication, which commemorated the Maccabean victory over the pagan Greeks in 167 B.C.

8. (pl. insulae) A family household arrangement common in Capernaum and Korazin, where many rooms—residences for various family members—were built around a central courtyard.

"There's someone you must meet!" Shim'on said, ignoring the jibe and clasping El'azar's arm eagerly. "He may be the answer to all our problems. He may be the Messiah."

El'azar rolled his eyes. "Not another one!" he exclaimed. How many had already claimed to be the promised Messiah—all of them, in the end, proving to be madmen or deceivers. And the only result had been the slaughter of their followers and additional Roman oppression. The people of Gamla knew this better than most.

"Yeshua[9] isn't like the others," Shim'on said, his dark eyes gazing earnestly at El'azar. "He's like no one we've ever met or heard before, El'azar. He's a rabbi. He has been teaching in the synagogue, and he talks about the 'good news of the kingdom.' I don't know what his plans are yet, but he is attracting followers."

"Impossible!" said one of the men. "This new rabbi may speak of the kingdom, but he also says we're to pray for our enemies—even love them! That's not going to drive out the Romans."

"I agree. But he intrigues me. Yeshua also says that no one can serve two masters," said Shim'on.

"Which one is he?" asked El'azar, nodding toward a group of men gathered in front of the synagogue.

"He's not here now. But he'll be teaching this afternoon on one of the hillsides outside town." Shim'on touched El'azar's shoulder to turn him around. "See those two arguing over there? The tall one is Kefa,[10] and the other is his brother. They were the first ones in town to meet Yeshua. He asked them to join his band. The sons of Zavdai,[11] the two over there looking at that olive press, were enlisted next. They're all fishermen—make a nice living here."

"I've never heard of any of them. Are they loyal to the movement?"

"Not as far as I can tell. Kefa's always sounding off about something, but he seems more concerned about his daily catch than the Roman dogs."

"If they don't believe in the cause, why are they following this Yeshua?" El'azar asked.

"His teaching has become very popular, and news of him is spreading fast and far. I'm surprised you haven't heard of him."

"Probably because there's so much going on. Some of our brothers have been escalating the conflict with their terrorism. They've been burning Roman

---

9. Jesus
10. Peter
11. Zebedee

haystacks and poisoning Roman wells. And the Romans have arrested Bar-Talmai [12] for knifing a Sadducee."

"Hah!" barked someone. "In the dark, the Romans and Sadducees all look alike!"

"But what good will Bar-Talmai do our movement when he's hanging on a Roman cross?" asked Shim'on.

"Death is better than slavery," said another.

"Yes, yes, that's what we've always believed. But so much blood and still no freedom—I'm beginning to wonder."

"What does this rabbi say?" asked El'azar.

"That we can serve only God. Yet he also says we won't need our knives anymore," said Shim'on. "I'm not sure about his methods, but I am sure he's passionate about the kingdom."

H ours later, after Yeshua had finished his long teaching session, El'azar sat on the hillside watching the crowd dwindle away.

What should I do? he wondered.

The day after tomorrow, he was supposed to be in Yerushalayim. [13] Bar-Abba, [14] one of their most zealous leaders, was looking for volunteers to help with a plot he was hatching. El'azar could hardly believe it when he got the message that he was needed by Bar-Abba, a man of great daring who would attempt anything—and somehow had never been caught.

Still, after hearing this rabbi's teaching and interpretation, El'azar knew why Shim'on was excited. The man's passion was compelling. But his message was confusing, puzzling, contradictory.

"Love your enemies. Pray for those who persecute you." Such ideas could not live alongside their creed. His father might brand him a traitor for even listening—like the Roman-loving Sadducees and Temple officials.

What should he do? Should he go on to Yerushalayim or stay here for a while and question the rabbi?

If it was only a matter of what he believed, it would be so much simpler. But how many had already died, misled by false messiahs? Would this one, too, along with his followers, end up on a Roman cross?

Was this Yeshua just another false messiah who would dash their hopes? Or

---

12. Bartholomew; *Bar* means "son of."
13. Jerusalem
14. Barabbas; *Bar* means "son of."

had God at last sent the leader their cause needed? Should he follow him and find out?

Serve no one but God.
Slavery is worse than death.
God created us to be free.
I owe allegiance to God alone.
No one can serve two masters.

That was the Zealots' creed.

While most of Jesus' Galilean ministry took place within an area of three and a half miles of a triangle cornered by Bethsaida, Korazin, and Capernaum, the entire countryside around the Sea of Galilee was of great significance. The southwestern shore was the home of the Herodians—the pro-Roman, secular Jews. The northwestern corner and north shore were where the religious Jews had gathered, home of Peter and Andrew, James and John, and the other disciples—the land of the 12. Across the lake, on the northeastern heights, was Zealot country, refuge of the Jewish terrorists dedicated to driving out the Romans. And on the southeastern side was "the other side"—pagan country, the Decapolis. The amazing thing is that these people could all see each other easily from their vantage points around the Sea of Galilee.

Yet they were separated by more than water. They were divided by racial hatred, politics, and religion.

Where people lived and how they lived was consistent with their theology. Fiercely independent, bound by a code of hatred, and isolated from the mainstream Jewish culture, the Zealots made their headquarters at the stronghold of Gamla.

The Zealots hated the Roman presence in their land and proved it by taking up the sword. In A.D. 67, thirty years after Jesus' death, the Romans besieged Gamla, destroyed the city, and killed most of its inhabitants, who held out till the end—a tragic scenario that would be repeated a few years later at Masada, its counterpart in the south, beside the Dead Sea. Ultimately, the Zealot movement ended in defeat and death, leaving only the blood of its followers in the dust.

A number of Zealots may have been among Jesus' followers, most for the wrong reasons. His messianic claim was not an uncommon one in that day. In previous generations, many men had claimed to be the Messiah, so "Oh no, not another one" wasn't a surprising response. To those who followed Jesus for political gain, He was just another option—a way to achieve their goal. The Zealots didn't understand that the method they chose was not Jesus' method. They wanted to reclaim their land, their world, with acts of terrorism; God wants to reclaim His world through human beings who love His Son.

Ultimately, this misunderstanding and the Zealots' method would bring Jesus to tears on the Mount of Olives:

> *If you, even you, had only known on this day what would bring you peace—but now it is hidden from your eyes. The days will come upon you when your enemies will build an embankment against you and encircle you and hem you in on every side. They will dash you to the ground, you and the children within your walls. They will not leave one stone on another, because you did not recognize the time of God's coming to you.*
>
> (Luke 19:42–44)

For the Zealot, there was no room for the paradox of faith: Serve only one master; love your enemies, and pray for those who persecute you.

Though we must serve only our Lord, we do so by loving others—even those who don't serve Him. We must have the passion of the Zealots and the method of the Messiah.

Understanding this helps us recognize why Jesus so frequently chose to hide His identity as the Messiah. So many in His immediate community misunderstood the nature of the Messiah, believing He would use violent military power to bring about the kingdom of God. That certainly included the Zealots, who believed use of the sword was the God-ordained battle plan. Contrast their chosen method with the "battle plan" Jesus presented for the coming of His kingdom.

Many people today think like the Zealots. Whether as murderers of government leaders or abortion doctors, as hostage-takers or snipers, as suicide bombers or torturers, fundamentalists of every religion believe God wants them to use violence.

Jesus said, "No, that's not the way. Love your enemies. Pray for those who persecute you. Welcome the children. Touch the leper. Bring the message of forgiveness to the prostitute and the tax collector. Visit the prisoner. Feed the hungry. Clothe the naked. Comfort the lonely and the mourning. Be salt. Be light!

"This," said Jesus, "is where the kingdom of God is happening, and this is the method by which I will bring My kingdom." And He then demonstrated this by going to a Roman cross. The King of the world, who could have called an army of angels to serve and protect Him, chose instead to serve those in need and to eternally save every human being who seeks the forgiving power of His sacrificial death and resurrection.

Likewise, if we're to become like our Rabbi, we must begin thinking as He thought and acting as He acted. We must be seen and known in the world as those who practice that kind of compassion, love, and self-sacrifice.

Jesus convincingly rejected the practices of the Zealot, although He was no less committed to truth and righteousness. No one was more passionate than our Lord, but His battle plan and method were unique.

For Yeshua, our Jewish Teacher and Messiah, it is the merciful and the peacemaker who bring truth, righteousness, and justice by being the salt of the earth and the light of the world.

Chapter 9

The Decapolis

Then Jesus left the vicinity of Tyre and went through Sidon, down to the Sea of Galilee and into the region of the Decapolis [the Ten Cities].

(Mark 7:31)

They went across the lake to the region of the Gerasenes [Gadarenes]. When Jesus got out of the boat, a man with an evil spirit came from the tombs to meet him. . . . He shouted at the top of his voice, "What do you want with me, Jesus, Son of the Most High God? Swear to God that you won't torture me!"

(Mark 5:1–2,7)

Jesus asked him, "What is your name?"
"Legion," he replied, because many demons had gone into him. And they begged him repeatedly not to order them to go into the Abyss.
A large herd of pigs was feeding there on the hillside. The demons begged Jesus to let them go into them, and he gave them permission. When the demons came out of the man, they went into

the pigs, and the herd rushed down the steep bank into the lake and was drowned. . . .

The man . . . begged to go with him, but Jesus sent him away, saying, "Return home and tell how much God has done for you."

(Luke 8:30–33,38–39a)

When they found him on the other side of the lake, they asked him, "Rabbi, when did you get here?"

Jesus answered, "I tell you the truth, you are looking for me, not because you saw miraculous signs but because you ate the loaves and had your fill. Do not work for food that spoils, but for food that endures to eternal life, which the Son of Man will give you. On him God the Father has placed his seal of approval."

Then they asked him, "What must we do to do the works God requires?"

Jesus answered, "The work of God is this: to believe in the one he has sent."

(John 6:25–29)

Galilee, A.D. 28

The man struggled against the chains that bound his wrists and ankles—clawed at them until his hands were bloody. His captors would not hold him here. His enemies were coming for him. He must escape!

"Pull harder, men. I'd like to beat that storm," Z'vulun[1] called to his oarsmen. The men stretched their backs like bows bent for shooting. Z'vulun could feel the east wind on his shoulders, blowing off the Gaulanitis, the heights above the northeastern shore of the lake. Already he could see the white foam spitting in the wind.

Today they were transporting grain from the docks at Hippos across the lake to the wharves at Tiberias. If the storm lasted, they'd have to wait it out, unless he could pick up a load for his return trip. Without the ballast of cargo, the barge could easily be swamped.

Business was good. Z'vulun seldom had to make a return trip with an empty hold. Still, he was always happier to be carrying cargo to Tiberias on the western side of the lake rather than making the return trip to the wharves below the high, fortified city of Hippos, the city the Jews called Sussita because it looked like the neck of a horse. Hippos was the main shipping point on the eastern side, in the Decapolis. Even as a dispassionate seaman and merchant, Z'vulun felt the stigma of the far side of Gennesaret.[2] Recently, his uneasiness had been magnified by some incidents at the docks. Whenever they tied up, they had been greeted by a crazy man.

"Why does this man attack us?" Z'vulun had asked. No one knew.

"He lives in the caves and the tombs outside town," some of the dock workers told him.

"He is possessed by demons!" said others.

---

1. Zebulun
2. The Sea of Galilee; also known as the Sea of Tiberias after Herod Antipas's capital city, Tiberias, which he named for his friend the Roman emperor Tiberius.

All one could see of the madman's face were his wild, insane eyes peering through his long, filthy, matted hair. His dirty body was covered with cuts and sores. His words often sounded like gibberish, and he sometimes became so violent that he was dangerous. They said he had injured and even killed people who crossed his path.

Perhaps such things shouldn't have been shocking, given the nature of this land, so different from Z'vulun's own, though only seven and a half miles across the water.

The Hellenistic cities of the Decapolis enjoyed freedoms other cities did not. Their theaters produced the latest obscene plays; their hippodromes and coliseums were filled with spectators for the naked athletic events and cruel, bloody, to-the-death gladiatorial and animal games relished by the Romans; and their temples and religious festivals displayed all the depravity of their gods and goddesses.

The Decapolis had been founded by Alexander the Great about 300 years before, in his attempt to plant Greek paganism around the world. After he conquered the land of Israel, he and his followers tried to force their Hellenistic worldview on the Jewish people. Those who resisted suffered terribly. Their sufferings were still remembered on Hanukkah, the feast that celebrated the Jews' deliverance from the Greeks by Y'hudah[3] Maccabee.

Then, nearly 100 years before, Pompey, the Roman conqueror who brought Israel into his empire, revived the cities of the Decapolis and joined them together in an alliance of city-states. Since then, they had become stronger and more pagan, a land of Gentiles in the midst of Jewish believers.

This land on the other side of Gennesaret had long been considered evil, however—even before the Greeks and Romans. When Israel conquered Canaan and drove out the pagan inhabitants, the rabbis said, seven pagan nations settled in the Gaulanitis. That was why some still called it "the land of the seven."[4] These were the descendants of those despised worshipers of Baal, with their perverted sexual practices, child sacrifices, and Asherah worship. The rabbis taught that in Baal worship, they sacrificed pigs to their gods—pigs, the symbol of evil.

The rabbis referred to these descendants of the Canaanites as the *gerusim*— the "driven-out ones," "the expelled ones." No wonder many were demon-possessed, these offspring of Baal-Zebub, the prince of baals.

Z'vulun wasn't afraid for himself, but the commotion the demoniac caused

---

3. Judah
4. Acts 13:19

interfered with their loading and unloading, and his horrifying appearance upset the more superstitious in the crew. Z'vulun himself had sailed the Mediterranean as a young man, before he had saved enough to establish his own shipping firm, and he had never seen such a superstitious lot as the sailors who sailed the great waters. But even on this small inland lake, with its violent storms and treacherous waves, many believed in omens and signs. Some said evil spirits lived in the depths.

His people, of course—the religious Jews of Galilee—didn't believe such things. In that regard and many others, Z'vulun was thankful for the faith of his fathers. For one thing, it kept him from having to transport the smelly swine of the pagans. He might have been forced to learn their language in order to do business, since the Greek-speaking Gentiles in the Decapolis refused to speak Hebrew and rarely spoke Aramaic, but Z'vulun refused to transport their pigs. He also refused to change his name and customs, unlike many of the other Jewish businessmen in the area. They tried to disguise themselves as Gentiles while still holding to their religious faith.

"Almost there, Captain," shouted his mate as they pulled into the shallows. In minutes, the deckhands had the barge tied up to the pilings at one of the wharves lining the waterfront of the glittering city of Tiberias.

"Shalom, Z'vulun," a friendly voice greeted him heartily as he stepped off the gangplank.

"Good to see you, Titus. How are you?"

Though the man was a Gentile, the two had become friends. Titus's hometown was Hippos, but since he had expanded his leather-goods business, he had moved to Tiberias, where the tourist trade brought more demand.

Z'vulun's heart ached for the man. What a sad life he'd had in recent years! His youngest son had rebelled against his father and left home. Titus talked about his son often, fretting over where he might be, worrying about what might have happened to him. That amazed Z'vulun. A Jewish father would have cut off such a rebellious child, disowned him, never spoken of him again, and considered him dead. But not Titus.

"If I could just see him," Titus said sadly, "just know where he is and that he's alive and well." Then he had clasped Z'vulun's arm and said, "Watch out for him in your travels, will you, my friend?"

Z'vulun had promised, but he'd never so much as caught a glimpse of the young man.

Often Titus left his busy shop to come down and meet Z'vulun here. Z'vulun knew he was always hoping for word of his son.

"I haven't seen him," Z'vulun said now, after the initial greetings were over. "I promise you I always look."

"Thank you, Z'vulun," said Titus. "I know you do. And I'm more grateful than you know." He paused for a moment, gazing toward the distant shore, then called his thoughts back. "Looks like heavy cargo this time."

"It is. They've had a good crop of grain this year in the heights." The flat, fertile fields high above the eastern shore of Gennesaret were farmed mostly by Gentiles, many of whom still worshiped their fertility gods. While the secular Jews in Tiberias and the Judean countryside were eager to buy the grain, the religious Jews refused. They would starve rather than eat bread made from the wheat raised by pagans.

"The crowds are heavy in the city," Titus said as the two walked toward the dockmaster's office. Tiberias was known not only for its cultural attractions, but also for its natural hot springs, thought to have healing waters. "Good for business."

"The city isn't the only thing drawing crowds," said Z'vulun. "I understand there's a rabbi up around Capernaum who's been attracting a lot of attention."

"Why would a rabbi draw a crowd?" asked Titus.

"He's pretty controversial. His interpretations of the Torah[5] have raised many questions. And yesterday I heard that he'd even traveled to 'the other side'[6] of Gennesaret."

"That is a bit odd, isn't it?"

Z'vulun nodded. "Not only a bit odd, but our rabbis teach that we must never be involved with those Gentile pagans. I've been criticized for even shipping their wheat."

No religious Jew would participate in such trade. But a rabbi going to "the other side"! That was unheard of. The other side of Galilee was the home of pagans, pigs, Gentiles—and Romans, no less. No wonder the demons lived there.

The pain in his head drove him crazy. The pictures in his mind made him wild. If only these demonic voices would go away and leave him alone. He looked down at his hands. Bloody. Had he cut himself or someone else? He couldn't remember.

---

5. The five books of Moses. The word *Torah* means "teachings," although it's often translated as "law."

6. Also known as the Decapolis; the area on the eastern side of the Sea of Galilee and the Jordan River that included a confederation of self-ruled Hellenistic cities.

What an assignment!" Marcus said to Gaius. "We were fortunate to be posted here."

The two muscular, leather-faced soldiers stood on the rampart atop the city wall edging the steep cliff. Far below, they could see the busy wharves here on the eastern shore of the Sea of Tiberias. Behind them was the well-fortified city of Hippos, just one of the places guarded by troops from their legion, the fifteenth Roman legion, stationed in this province.

Their banner, bearing the insignia of the wild boar, waved colorfully and proudly above the colonnaded main street that stretched straight across the city to the main eastern gate. Though the city was accessible here on the western side, this gate was used primarily by the soldiers, by slaves lugging goods up the steep switchback trail from the docks, and by farmers who worked the terraced mountainside and the fertile plain below, with its fruit and olive trees.

Most of the citizens lived in villages outside the walls, but daily they filled the city's marketplace, did business in its public buildings, enjoyed drama in its theater, and used the water provided by its 20-mile-long aqueduct that ended in a huge public fountain, which then flowed into the city's cisterns. What a choice assignment! Hundreds of red granite columns lined the streets. The floors of the shops were exquisitely shaded and colored mosaics.

"I'd rather be here than over there," Gaius said, nodding toward the city across the lake. "Tiberias has its attractions, but it's too close to all those religious Jews."

"A troublemaking lot," agreed Marcus.

As they watched the barge traffic and fishing vessels on the clear, blue water, the two men talked about the recent escalation in Zealot activities in Yerushalayim.[7] That, along with the flurry surrounding another would-be messiah attracting followers in Galilee, had increased the need for vigilance on the part of the Roman troops.

"I'm glad we're here and not in Yerushalayim," said Marcus. "Or on a crucifixion detail."

"The way things are going, we'll probably see that duty sooner or later," said Gaius.

"Later is fine with me. I don't enjoy torture. A swift stroke of the sword is the way to kill an enemy."

---

7. Jerusalem

Running. Stumbling. His head pounding. The voices shrieking. He'd only wanted food.
He'd managed to steal scraps from the swine pens until the herders drove him off. Now he
was so hungry and weak that he could barely walk. Still, the demons drove him on.

arcus's peaceful watch came to an end suddenly the next morning when
he was ordered down to the harbor just to the south. The centurion had
said, "Some Jewish insurrectionist and his followers came across the lake
last night, and crowds are gathering to hear him. Get down there and keep the
peace. Do whatever you have to do to keep order." Now here were Marcus and
his men, patrolling the rocky shore.

According to the rumors, a Jewish rabbi and several of his followers had
crossed the lake and immediately been attacked by one of the madmen who
inhabited local caves and tombs. This one was so violent that he had even been
chained up at times, but somehow he always broke loose. Instead of fighting
him off or calling for help, this rabbi had cured the man, it was said. Rumor had
it that he had driven the demons out of him.

While Marcus and his men were investigating this, another problem arose.
The leaders of the nearby town rushed up to them in an absolute frenzy.

"Our entire herd of pigs, over 2,000 valuable animals belonging to the
temples of Zeus, Hera, and Tyche,[8] rushed off the cliff into the sea and drowned!"
they said. "And it's that rabbi's fault! He's to blame! He stampeded them!"

Then one of the soldiers reported angrily to Marcus that the man who was
"possessed by demons" had called his demons "Legion." "Is that some deroga-
tory reference to our legion insignia?" the soldier asked. "Is this some attempt to
dishonor us?"

What kind of nonsense is this? Marcus wondered. *Is everyone over here crazy?*
Maybe it's something in the water.

The townspeople had been so upset that they had demanded that the rabbi
leave the area. Apparently, he hadn't argued. He and his students had gotten into
their boat and sailed back to the western shore.

But the madman was still here, the town leaders said, "dressed and sane."

What in the world was the explanation for this? Marcus wondered. If this
man had access to some god, it certainly wasn't one of the Roman pantheon.
Their gods had been known to interfere in times past, but they didn't anymore.
Besides, gods never bothered with individuals. What kind of god would do
something like this?

---

8. Gods from the Greek pantheon

He walked down the street, looking for someone who hadn't heard his miraculous story. Those who knew him, of course, were astonished by the change in his appearance. What they couldn't see was the change inside. His mind was clear. His heart still pounded, but now with joy! No more voices. No more nightmares. No more rage and anger. No more fear. He was free.

He had begged to go with the teacher, but the teacher said no.

"Return home and tell how much God has done for you," the teacher had said.

So he'd been doing just that. Whenever he did, people crowded around, even those who had heard the story. Many seemed to want to hear it again and again, just as they did now as he began to tell what the rabbi had done for him.

Suddenly, over the heads of the crowd, he recognized a gray-haired man coming toward him. They hadn't spoken for . . . how long had it been since he'd been in his right mind? How long since the demons overtook him?

"Z'vulun! Shalom!" he called.

"Is that you?" Z'vulun said. "I don't believe it!"

"It is."

"Is it possible?" said his father's old friend, his eyes bright with tears.

"Believe your eyes, Z'vulun."

"Your father has been sick with worry. Where have you been all this time? What have you been doing? I've heard rumors about demons. What's happened?"

"Let me tell you about it," he said.

Though we might expect that Jesus, like other religious Jews of His day, would have isolated Himself from the pagan world around Him, the opposite was true. Jesus not only set up the headquarters of His ministry within easy walking or sailing distance of those people, but He also, on several occasions, deliberately attempted to minister to the pagan communities of the Decapolis.

There's quite a lesson in that. It's relatively easy to be a Christian witness within our own comfort zone—to people who look, dress, act, talk, and think like us. It becomes much more difficult when we move out into the larger world to bring the message, the example, and the insights of Jesus to our culture—to people whose values, morals, and lifestyles are different, often distressingly so, from our own.

Yet Jesus' message isn't just for those who are sympathetic or who already understand it—or think they do.

When Jesus went to the Decapolis, He immediately confronted the power of Satan. Just the fact that He visited that area was astounding, considering its pagan reputation. That was where Baal-Zebub reigned supreme. So Jesus not only was willing to bring His message to those whose values, beliefs, and lifestyles were totally opposed to His own, but He also directly confronted the very heart of evil, the devil himself.

Again, there's a lesson here. In our world, it's easy as Christians to assume that those areas that seem clearly under the influence of the power of evil are off-limits, as if they are places where Christians should never live, work, or witness. Many of us avoid, therefore, such arenas as the secular media, Hollywood, Madison Avenue, and popular music. In the process, while we try to stay "safe" in our little world, we also ignore such difficult issues as racism, poverty, and violence.

In his book *Roaring Lambs*,[9] Bob Briner made a passionate appeal for the Christian community to encourage its young people to become involved in the writing and production of movies, television programs, plays, and popular music; in the editing of newspapers and magazines; in journalism and the arts. If we're going to be salt and light, we must bring our influence to that which shapes our culture, even if they're areas that have been used for evil in the past.

The power of God can transform the greatest evil. When Jesus went to the Decapolis and healed the demon-possessed man, sending the demons into the pigs and, through them, into the abyss, the man was powerfully changed. The demons were gone; his life was healed, and he became a new creation. Translating this into our own cultural context, we can say that even the abortionist, the pornographer, the drug dealer, and the murderer can be changed by the power of God. But we must bring them to God—or bring God to them.

After Jesus had healed the man, He issued a challenge: "Now that you've been changed, go home and tell your world." Jesus didn't exhort him to learn the latest theological trend or establish the five points of his theology. Instead He said, "Go tell them what God has done for you." Simple . . . yet profound.

Sometime later, when Jesus was on His way to Jerusalem to die, He traveled by way of the Decapolis, through the very territory where He had healed the demon-possessed man. There He was met by a crowd of believers. I have often

---

wondered whether it was the simple witness of that one man who had experienced a life-changing encounter with Jesus that produced that kind of fruit. I think it's not only possible but even probable. If one man could so influence a very pagan community, imagine the impact you could have telling others what God has done for you!

The biggest barrier to Christian witness is the assumption that it is a theological exercise demanding specialized knowledge and practiced technique. Technique is valuable. Theological knowledge and biblical literacy are important. But the key to being a follower of Jesus is simply a willingness to tell others what God has done for you.

Chapter 10

The Living Water

My people have committed two sins: They have forsaken me,
the spring of living water, and have dug their own cisterns, broken
cisterns that cannot hold water.

(Jeremiah 2:13)

Jesus answered, "Everyone who drinks this water will be thirsty
again, but whoever drinks the water I give him will never thirst.
Indeed, the water I give him will become in him a spring of water
welling up to eternal life."

(John 4:13–14)

On the last and greatest day of the Feast [of Sukkot], Jesus
stood and said in a loud voice, "If anyone is thirsty, let him come to
me and drink. Whoever believes in me, as the Scripture has said,
streams of living water will flow from within him."

(John 7:37–38)

Can both fresh water and salt water flow from the same spring?

(James 3:11)

The Judean Wilderness, A.D. 29

hirst gripped Asher's throat, as did his fear of jackals and other foes too dreadful to name. Here at the remote southern end of the Salt Sea,[1] where Jahweh's anger had destroyed the cities of Sodom and Gomorrah centuries before, a strange sense of evil gripped him. He dared not think about the evil of those towns now buried beneath him.

Though he had worked at the mines in Zoar for almost two years, he had always traveled up the western side of the Judean Mountains, through Hebron and north to Yerushalayim,[2] avoiding this more direct but desolate route through the wilderness. Now he remembered why, but it was too late to turn back. The eerie loneliness of the wind-carved passages through the salt mountains closed in on him and terrified him.

A short time later, he escaped the salt mountains and his nameless terror, only to plunge into another barren landscape: the immense mountains and deep wadis of the Judean Wilderness.

As Asher walked north under the burning sun, with the mountains to his left and the Salt Sea to his right, his parched tongue demanded water. But he knew he had to drink sparingly from his waterskin. Salt-encrusted rocks and ghostly, stunted fingers of dead trees lined the shore of the sea. The bright, blue water beyond looked clean and refreshing, but he knew it was only a mirage. Drinking that thick, salty liquid would kill the drinker but not his thirst.

Yesterday, after he left the bitumen mines at Zoar and began his hot, dry, lonely trek, Asher had passed few travelers, though he was occasionally comforted by the distant presence of nomadic shepherds guarding their camels, goats, and sheep. He was amazed that their animals could eke sustenance from the tiny, green shoots that sprang up almost individually from ground that, from a distance, looked arid and lifeless.

---

1. Dead Sea
2. Jerusalem

Yet loneliness was preferable to the sign of habitation he now saw on the horizon: a huge, flat-topped mountain of rock housing a Roman fortress. He would give it wide berth.

Asher walked warily, looking around constantly, as the mountain loomed larger and larger. As he drew even with it, though it was still some distance to the west, he could see the fortress on top, where soldiers guarded Judea's southern frontier from its enemies. Down the northern face of the plateau marched the three tiers of Herod's colorful hanging palace. The beauty and the company held no attraction for Asher. If he could avoid any encounters with the soldiers of Rome, he would do so.

To the Jewish people, this masada[3] had deep significance. But like everything else in their land, Herod and the Romans had claimed it.

King Daveed[4] had sung of a desert fortress, probably this very one, that had sheltered him from the hand of Saul: "The LORD is my rock, my fortress and my deliverer; my God is my rock, in whom I take refuge."[5] Asher prayed those words now, hoping for his own safety and deliverance from harm.

As a faithful Jew, Asher meditated on the God of his fathers night and day and always put the Law first. That was why he was making this trip to Yerushalayim instead of earning shekels[6] at the bitumen mines. He might have left his father's home up north in the Soreq Valley, but he had not left his God.

Looking at his bleak surroundings, Asher thought of his family and the beautiful, broad, fertile valley where he had been born and raised. There, where Shimshon[7] had faced the Philistines and Daveed had killed Goliath, a variety of temptations still confronted the followers of Jahweh. The coastal plain, near the Shephelah[8] where his family lived, was populated with Hellenistic pagans, especially the cities of Ashdod and Ashkelon. Many of Asher's own people, like Shimshon, had fallen under that pagan influence and strayed onto paths of sin.

Jahweh required faithfulness amid even the greatest temptations and pressures of life, which was why Asher had left his work and was making this pilgrimage through the wilderness. Every Jewish male, the Law commanded, must attend the three great feasts in Yerushalayim: Passover and Shavuot[9] in the

---

3. Fortress
4. David
5. Psalm 18:2
6. A coin used to pay the Temple tax.
7. Samson
8. The foothills between the coastal plain on the Mediterranean and the Judean Mountains.
9. Means "weeks"; also known as Pentecost or the Feast of Weeks. It's celebrated 50 days after the Sabbath following Passover.

Living Water. The waterfall at the oasis of En Gedi in the Judean Wilderness turns the desert into a lush paradise. The water flows from several springs located a few hundred feet beyond the falls. (*Ray Vander Laan*)

spring, and Sukkot [10] in the fall. Asher had never missed one, and he was determined to be in Yerushalayim in time for Sukkot, the most joyous of all their sacred days—the only feast at which Jahweh had commanded His people to "rejoice before him." [11]

The significance of the upcoming feast struck Asher anew as he gazed at the wilderness around him. Although Sukkot was the Jews' annual time of thanksgiving for the plentiful harvest of fruit, wine, and olive oil, the feast was also

---

10. Also known as the Feast of Tabernacles or Booths. It took place in late fall.
11. Leviticus 23:40

intended to remind them that their forefathers had dwelt in tents in the wilderness after Jahweh had brought them safely out of Egypt.

To live 40 years in a place like this, Asher thought, licking his dry lips. *I'm thankful I don't have to do that.*

He slung the waterskin off his shoulder and held the neck to his mouth, hoping to squeeze out a few more drops. The pouch would soon be as dry as the salty dust on his skin. Yesterday, he had filled it at the cistern before he left Zoar. The water had smelled stale, and there had been debris floating on the surface. Still, it was drinkable, and he longed for it now.

At the nomad encampment where he had been welcomed and spent last night, the men had told him marvelous tales of an oasis north of the mountains of salt, a place called En Gedi, though they had also warned him about the huge, wild cats that roamed there. As Asher listened, he'd remembered the stories of King Daveed and how the great ruler had fled for his life and hidden in the caves near the springs of En Gedi.

Suddenly, as though conjured by his thoughts, a column of green appeared on the horizon. Before long, the dark color distinguished itself into palm trees, irrigated fields, and vineyards. *This must be the plantation owned by the Herod family,* Asher thought. He had heard of the succulent dates and sweet perfume that came from their palm and balsam plantations. As he walked through the groves of date palms, he saw workers in the distance, but no one approached him or inquired about his business.

How much better it would be to work in this oasis settlement than at the harsh mines of Zoar—and it would be miles closer to Yerushalayim, Asher thought. He could see they even had a synagogue in which to pray. Perhaps after Sukkot he could return here and find work.

The fields and groves gradually gave way to a long, winding canyon. Wild and uncultivated, though alive with trees and tall, grassy reeds, this wadi crawled up into the hills. Rising above him on both sides were chalky-white cliffs pockmarked with shadowed caves. As he started up the wadi, the moist, green coolness immediately relieved the burning heat of the sun.

Something moved in the undergrowth, startling him. Holding his breath, he stopped and listened. He heard the panting of an animal, and, peering through the brush, he saw a deer coming out of the desert for water. Asher relaxed and moved on. He didn't fear the deer or the wild goats—only the leopard who hunted at night, or so the nomads had told him. He hoped they were right.

The climb grew steeper. Asher pulled himself over huge boulders and crawled through cool, damp passages of overhanging rocks. Suddenly, he heard a roaring noise. He moved cautiously around an outcropping of rock and stepped into a clearing—and looked up at the biggest torrent of water he had ever seen! Immediately in front of him, a veil of crystal spun down from the heights into a pool far below.

Asher gingerly found a foothold among rocks that were green with moss and damp with trickles of water. He reached out his hand and brought it back, wet, to his mouth. Cool. Clear. Saltless. *A spring in the desert,* like the words of the prophet that the rabbi read from the Yesha'yahu [12] scroll in the synagogue.

> *Each man will be like a shelter from the wind and a refuge from the storm, like streams of water in the desert and the shadow of a great rock in a thirsty land. . . .*
>
> *The desert and the parched land will be glad; the wilderness will rejoice and blossom. . . .*
>
> *Water will gush forth in the wilderness and streams in the desert. The burning sand will become a pool, the thirsty ground bubbling springs. In the haunts where jackals once lay, grass and reeds and papyrus will grow.* [13]

How much better this living water is than the stale, dirty water I drew from the cistern, Asher thought. *No wonder the prophet wrote that worshiping other gods is like drinking cistern water when there's a spring nearby. And no wonder our rabbi says that trying to live by your own strength is like drinking from a cistern.*

Asher drank until his stomach hurt, then feasted on the round, flat bread [14] and small cakes of goat cheese the nomads had shared with him. His hunger satisfied and his thirst quenched, he climbed up the rocky ledges, looking for a place to spend the night.

At sunset, sheltered by one of the caves above the waterfall, Asher looked east, across the Salt Sea. Its waters were no longer the azure blue of the sky. The sun, sinking behind the Judean Mountains at his back, reflected from the red mountains of Moab and made the water look like blood.

Asher slept soundly that night. Knowing any animals in the area would go down to drink after sundown, he felt safe where he was, though he stayed far back in the cave so the wind would not catch his scent and carry it to them.

In the morning, he started north once more, plunging from the cool, green

---

12. Isaiah
13. Isaiah 32:2; 35:1,6–7
14. Thin, flat bread that can be separated easily into two layers to form a pocket; also known as pita bread.

oasis into the heat of the sun. The path was still rocky and dusty, but his water-skin was full of clean water. He had rinsed it well and filled it from the clear, flowing spring.

By midday, Asher could see the Essene settlement of Qumran perched high on a plateau to his left beneath the mountains. A year or two ago, when he had celebrated his eighteenth birthday and wondered whether to continue farming with his father in the fertile fields below their village of Azekah or to seek his livelihood elsewhere, Asher had thought about joining this sect of Sadducees. They had left the Temple establishment in Yerushalayim to devote themselves to studying Scripture and preparing to be the new priesthood when the Messiah arrived.

At first, what Asher heard about the Essenes attracted him. They lived communally and raised all their own food and provisions; they would touch nothing that hadn't been prepared by their own hands. Their self-containment and devotion to Jahweh appealed to him as the perfect way to shut out the world and live a holy life, something he longed to do. But as he spoke about this with the rabbi at their local synagogue and with his father and two brothers, Asher began to realize that this way of life was not for him. Life, even a life obedient to Jahweh, must be more than retreat and entrenchment.

In the distance, he could see the aqueduct that the Essenes had constructed to bring water from the wadi down to the complex water installations in their settlement. Water was essential for survival in the wilderness, but it was also an important part of the Essenes' religious life. They were meticulous about cere-monial cleanness, performing their ablutions daily, and ceremonial cleansing required living water—water that ran freely, not the stored, stale water of wells or cisterns, nor the salt-laden water of the nearby sea.

Having just been to En Gedi, Asher thought he now understood why Jahweh required living water for purification. Anyone who could dig a well or carve out a cistern could store rainwater or seepage. But only Jahweh could provide fresh, flowing, living water, and only Jahweh could provide the purity ceremonial cleansing symbolized.

Now that he thought about it, Asher remembered hearing that one of the Essenes had even left the community and was baptizing people in the Jordan River, preaching the coming of the Messiah and the need to be clean inside and out.

Three days and 30 miles later, after trekking as far north as Yericho[15] and then making the western climb up the Yericho Road, Asher arrived in Yerushalayim. The entire city was astir with preparations for the Feast of Sukkot. Thousands of pilgrims filled the streets, and sukkot[16] filled every available space, no matter how small. For one week, the Jews—even those who lived in Yerushalayim—would live, eat, and sleep in these shelters made of olive, palm, and myrtle branches.

Asher met up with his father and brothers near the home of Chanoch,[17] a cousin who lived in the street of the leather-makers. Asher had not seen his family since the spring, when they had all been in Yerushalayim for Shavuot, and he greeted them joyfully. One person was missing, though.

"Where is Mother?" Asher asked.

"She did not make the pilgrimage this time," said his father. "Your sister is betrothed now to Tehan, son of Telah. Your mother stayed at home to help her prepare for her wedding."

"Look," said Asher's elder brother, pointing to a stack of branches piled near the doorway of Chanoch's home. "We've brought all the supplies we need."

As they built the sukkah, Asher told his family about all he had seen in the past few days. They talked and laughed, glad to be together again.

They weren't alone in their happiness. Sukkot was always a joyous time, and laughter and singing filled the streets. The feast lasted for seven days, and as the week passed, the celebration became increasingly intense, almost frenzied. It happened every year. By the seventh day, Asher knew from experience, the Temple would be packed with pilgrims, and chants of praise would echo throughout the city and across the surrounding hills. Lulavs[18] by the thousands would beat the air, a vast sea of branches. The Pharisees had adopted this custom years ago, and it was now a joyous part of the celebration. Even the smallest children carried their own palm branches. And after the procession of priests had made the sacrifices and carried the wine and water to the altar for the drink offering, thousands would sing the great Hosannah as they waved their branches toward the altar: "O LORD, save us. O LORD, grant us success. Blessed is he who comes in the name of the LORD."[19]

When the sukkah was finished, Asher and his family began making their way

---

15. Jericho
16. (sing. sukkah) Booths made of olive, palm, and myrtle branches.
17. Enoch
18. A cluster of palm, myrtle, and willow branches tied together and waved during the Feast of Sukkot.
19. Psalm 118:25–26

to the Temple for the daily three o'clock sacrifice. Though the distance was not great, the crowds made for slow progress.

"There's a new teacher at the Temple," said Chanoch when they finally stepped onto Tyropean Street, the main north-south thoroughfare that ran along the western wall of the Temple Mount. Though the crowds were even greater here, it was wide enough that they could walk together and make themselves heard.

"Whenever you see two or more people huddled together, looking over their shoulders, you can be sure that's who they're discussing," said Asher's father.

"What's so strange about a new teacher?" asked Asher. "Every year or so, there's at least one we haven't seen before."

"This one is different," said his father. "Word in the streets is that the Sadducees at the Temple are furious about this man's interpretation of the Torah[20]—and especially about the strong following he has gained in Galilee."

"In Galilee!" Asher said with a laugh. "Who cares about that backward place?" Though Galilee was heavily populated and famous for its flour millstones, olive presses, and fishing industry, Asher knew that many considered the rural area to the north a land of uneducated laborers.

"Some are saying this teacher could be Messiah," replied his younger brother.

"Another one!" Asher snorted. "Many have claimed that title!"

"Well, he's certainly causing controversy," said his father. "Some say he's a good man. Others believe he's nothing more than a deceiver."

It isn't surprising that rumors of the Messiah should surface during this time, Asher thought. Since the days of Y'hudah[21] Maccabee and his great freedom fighters almost 200 years before, the palm branch had become the symbol of political as well as religious freedom for the Jewish people. Even coins now carried the palm branch, signifying the Jews' desire for political deliverance.

After Y'hudah cleansed the defiled Temple, he had reinstituted the Feast of Sukkot. Ever since then, the palms had become part of the celebration of the feast, and the great Hosannah chant—"Save us!"—had taken on additional meaning. Before, it had been sung in remembrance of their deliverance from Egypt and as a prayer for forgiveness and rain for next year's harvest. Now it had also become a prayer, a fervent plea, for political freedom, something the Jewish people had not known for more than 500 years.

Asher easily dismissed the rumors about the new teacher and settled in to enjoy the celebration and remember God's miraculous deliverance of their people.

---

20. The five books of Moses. The word *Torah* means "teachings," although it's often translated as "law."
21. Judah

A Mikveh. This ritual bath is located in the ruins of Qumran, probably the home of the Essenes. Immersion in its water symbolized ritual purity. The water had to be "living" water—water that flowed of its own accord. (*Eyal Bartov*)

On the fourth day of the feast, when the city was so crowded that a person could hardly move without bumping into someone's sukkah, an amazing thing happened. Asher and his brothers had just cleansed themselves in the living water that flowed through one of the many ritual baths at the bottom of the southern stairway to the Temple when their father shoved shoulders aside to push his way to them. He was excited and out of breath.

"I just heard someone say that the Galilean rabbi, Yeshua,[22] is teaching in the Temple courts," he said. "Let's go hear what he has to say."

"Is it safe?" asked Asher's younger brother. "I've heard that he's leading some kind of revolt and that the Pharisees want him silenced. It might be dangerous to be seen with him."

"If that were true, they wouldn't permit him to teach in the Temple," said their father. "Come. I want to hear him."

So Asher and his family made their way up the broad stairway. With thou-

---

22. Jesus

sands of pilgrims coming and going from the place of prayer and sacrifice, it took them some time to find the man they sought.

"Have you seen Yeshua, the rabbi from Galilee?" they kept asking. Bent on their own business, some ignored their inquiry. Of those who did answer, many didn't know who they were talking about. Finally, however, they reached the edge of a crowd gathered around the teacher, blocking the way and causing much yelling and comment from those trying to get past.

Pushed and pulled by the crowd, Asher got separated from his family, but he found a place in the audience. Soon he was captivated and amazed by the rabbi's words.

Fire flashed in Yeshua's dark eyes as he taught from a collection of parables about the kingdom of heaven. The Galilean even dared to criticize the Temple authorities for abusing their office. And Asher was astonished at the way he boldly rebuked some of the Pharisees for hypocrisy, pride, and ostentatious displays of religiosity.

Asher looked around uncomfortably to see if any Pharisees were in the crowd—and spotted a number of them. Some of these religious men nodded in agreement as they listened to the Galilean. Others looked ready to throw the teacher out of the Temple, and Asher could see them muttering among themselves.

When Yeshua was finished, Asher looked for his family in the crowd. As he did, he overheard several people saying they believed the man was Messiah. Asher didn't know what to think.

Before long Asher found himself swept up into the final days of the celebration. Since his recent experience in the desert, he sensed part of Sukkot taking on new meaning for him. The feast took place at the end of the dry season. The rains must begin soon or there would be no harvest next year. So part of the ceremony was always a prayer for rain, for God's living water.

This portion of Sukkot began on the last day, when a procession of priests marched from the Temple down to the Pool of Siloam, which was filled by the Spring of Gihon. One priest drew a golden pitcher of the living water, and the procession then returned to the Temple, just after the sacrifices were laid on the altar.

The priest carrying the water entered the priests' court through the Water Gate and, to the blast of the shofar, moved to the altar. Then, while the crowd and the Levitical choir sang the Hallel,[23] he circled the altar.

---

23. A selection comprising Psalms 113–118 and 135–136 chanted during Jewish feasts.

"Hosannah! Hosannah! Save us! Hosannah!" The sound was deafening. Thousands of pilgrims jammed the Temple courts, crying to God for life-giving rain. "Save us! Send us rain!" They waved their palm branches toward the altar as they cried, "Hosannah! Hosannah! Hosannah! Hosannah!"

Then, in an instant, the crowd grew silent, and with great solemnity, the priest poured the living water into one of the two silver funnels used for the daily drink offerings.

As the crowd became one huge mass pressing to get close to the altar, Asher found himself pushed toward a corner of the courtyard. Suddenly, he heard the strong, familiar voice of the Galilean rabbi. "If anyone is thirsty," he shouted, "let him come to me and drink."

Asher turned. Yeshua must have been sitting on a cage that had once held doves or pigeons, for it was overturned at his feet. But now he stood to deliver his message to the crowd.

"Whoever believes in me," he cried, "as the Scripture has said, streams of living water will flow from within him."

Living water! I know what that means, Asher thought. Living water, not cistern water. Water that brings life. He thought about the wilderness, about the springs at En Gedi, about the Sukkot prayers for rain and deliverance. *If his words are true, this man can only be from God, because living water can only come from God*, Asher thought.

"Come to me," Yeshua said. Asher pushed against the bodies around him. He must get closer. He must hear more.

Jesus chose the Feast of Sukkot, the time when the Israelites prayed to God for living water, to declare *Himself* the living water. He presented Himself to them as their most important source of life. In a land that's dry and dusty 10 months of the year, where every step is up or down hill, over rocks and under burning sun, thirst comes quickly. Without fresh water, life cannot exist.

For 40 years, the Israelites wandered in that barren land. But God went with them, and at each spot along the way, He provided water—sometimes out of the rocks themselves. Frequently, the Israelites had to drink from brackish pools or polluted cisterns. Then they would come to an oasis like En Gedi and find living water flowing clear and cold, forming a pool that sustained shade trees, plants, papyrus, and wildlife. Living water in the middle of the wilderness.

Over and over in His Word, God describes life as a wilderness, a place where the sun is brutal and water is scarce; a place where we become hot, dry, and thirsty—where we experience such trials as the death of a loved one, a broken relationship, a rebellious child, or physical or mental illness. How often, during those times, have we wished that God would say, "I'm going to remove the heat that's exhausting you. I'm going to take away the conditions that are causing your thirst. I'm going to make things easier."

But that's not usually His way. Instead, God says, "I will provide. When you're so overheated that you're about to faint, there'll be shade. When your tongue is so thick with thirst that it sticks to the roof of your mouth, there'll be water—just enough to make the heat of life's circumstances tolerable."

Water, of course, does more than quench our thirst. It also gives us life.

The Bible describes two kinds of water. First, there's cistern water, which is dirty runoff that collects after a rain. The prophet Jeremiah suggested that when we drink cistern water, we're seeking to satisfy our thirst in ways that aren't appropriate to God's design—we're honoring someone other than God. "They have left me, the spring of living water," Jeremiah said. "They have dug their own cisterns, broken cisterns that cannot hold water" (Jeremiah 2:13).

That's what life is like when we leave God and serve other gods. One way we do that is by trying to do something in our own strength instead of depending on the living water offered by God. That's like drinking dirty cistern water—or worse, water from the Dead Sea. The sparkling, blue waters of the Dead Sea look refreshing, but they're worthless when it comes to restoring life. What appears attractive and refreshing is often the very opposite. It will kill us.

Living water, however, is cool and clean. It's the refreshing, life-giving water that comes from seeking God and from being in relationship with Him. In the Judean Wilderness, God provided His people with En Gedi, an oasis of soothing shade, refreshing streams, and waterfalls spilling out of limestone rocks. God has also provided an En Gedi for us as we travel the hot, dry wilderness of life: His Son Jesus. Without Him, we'll die. He is our source of water and shade. Without Him, the scorching heat of everyday life would soon destroy us. Apart from Him, we simply can't make it. Thus, the time we spend with Jesus, nurturing our relationship with Him, is essential. It's the only thing that replenishes us so we have the strength to stay faithful to Him.

Eventually, we have to leave En Gedi, of course. We have to go out again into the wilderness of life—as did David and our Savior—and walk faithfully before

God. That's where our responsibilities are. But En Gedi is always there, and we can come back whenever we need to be refreshed, restored with life only God can give us.

Also, we can bring others to En Gedi. We can, in fact, become En Gedi to others in Jesus Christ, by bringing them His Word or being channels of His healing and restorative power.

How often do we go to En Gedi?

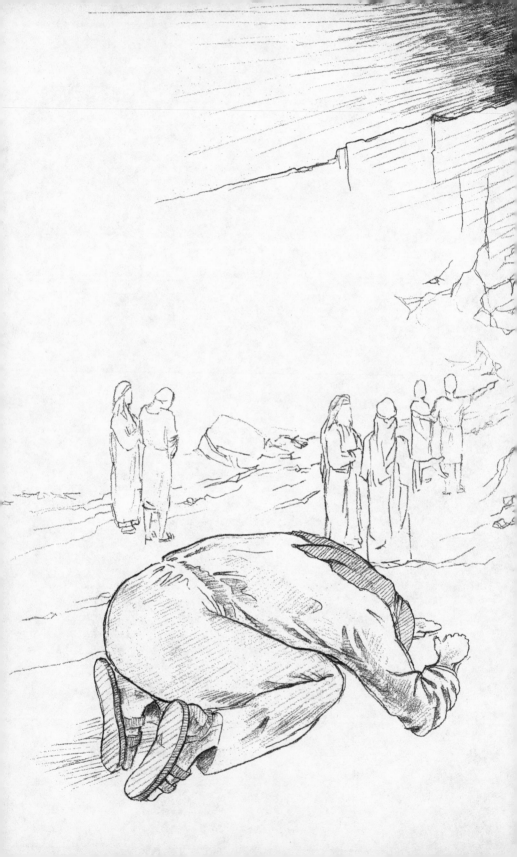

Part 3

What He Did

Chapter 11

The Jericho Road

They were on their way up to Jerusalem, with Jesus leading the way, and the disciples were astonished, while those who followed were afraid. Again he took the Twelve aside and told them what was going to happen to him. "We are going up to Jerusalem," he said, "and the Son of Man will be betrayed to the chief priests and teachers of the law. They will condemn him to death and will hand him over to the Gentiles, who will mock him and spit on him, flog him and kill him. Three days later he will rise."...

Then they came to Jericho.

(Mark 10:32–34,46a)

The Road from Jericho to Jerusalem, A.D. 30

Camels, donkeys, and sheep. Caravans and merchants. Vendors offering the sweet, succulent figs, dates, and pomegranates of Yericho.[1] Traders from the east and buyers from the west. Servants and noblemen. All crowded the busy streets of the oasis town.

With its groves of tall date palms and slender, stately cypress, Yericho rested like an emerald in the brown Judean foothills north of the Salt Sea.[2] Its verdant vegetation spread across the river plain, reaching toward the banks of the Jordan.

From all directions—north, south, east, and west—traffic passed through this crossroads on the west side of the river. Travelers coming out of the wilderness to the south, along the shores of the Salt Sea, welcomed Yericho's fresh springwater and cooling shade. Religious Jews from Galilee, to the north, usually traveled up to Yerushalayim[3] by way of Yericho. While it might be the long way around, it was the only way to avoid the dangers of going through Samaritan territory.

Hot and dry year-round, yet tempered and watered by the ever-gushing Spring of Elisha, Yericho boasted the winter palace of the Herods. Originally, this royal complex had belonged to the Hasmonaean kings, but Herod the Great had grabbed it, along with the throne.

Yochanan[4] thought about the king as he walked up the broad, shallow wadi that marked the beginning of the road to Yerushalayim, 17 miles away. At 19, he was too young to remember the first Herod, but the hated ruler and his bloody dynasty, now embodied in his son Herod Antipas, was still very much alive in the minds of Yochanan's people. As amazing as it seemed, some of the Herodians had even thought for a time that Herod was the Messiah—until he had died here in his palace at Yericho.

---

1. Jericho
2. Dead Sea
3. Jerusalem
4. John

The palace complex spread above Yochanan on both sides of the wadi. During Herod the Great's lifetime, the master builder had erected even more luxurious buildings and accommodations here, with lavish apartments and heated baths for himself and his guests. He also built a large swimming pool where, it was rumored, he had ordered the drowning of his own brother-in-law, the high priest Aristobulus.

Yochanan admired the marble columns of the poolside pavilion and the intricately patterned walls that surrounded elaborate sunken gardens. Herod had named this winter palace after the Roman emperor Augustus. Herod, and now his son Antipas, seemed determined to make Judea part of the Greek and Roman world, with its blasphemous glorification of humanity. Though the Jews might thwart the king's efforts at spreading the cult of emperor worship in their land, they had not been able to stop the spread of the Greek language or the proliferation of stadiums, temples, and theaters.

Soon after he passed the palace, Yochanan came to the place where the wadi deepened and narrowed and the land dropped away sharply on the left side of the road. Just ahead, at this natural gateway, he saw two Essenes standing well enough back that they would not make bodily contact with anyone, lest they become unclean. These pious desert men were known for their ascetic, celibate, and communal lifestyle. Garbed in frayed white robes, they presented a sharp contrast to the travelers streaming past them.

As he approached the two men, Yochanan realized they were talking to everyone who passed. "Leave the children of darkness," one cried. "Listen to the sons of light." Yochanan knew that was what they called themselves, the sons of light.

"Come into the wilderness," the other said. "Come await the Messiah."

"In the desert prepare for the Lord by living his way," the first cried. "Make a straight path in the wilderness for our God."

"We alone are living God's way. Join us. Help us prepare in the desert for the Lord by living His way."

Rendered uneasy by their entreaties and their invoking of the words of the great prophet Yesha'yahu,[5] Yochanan hurried past without looking at them. Such strange zeal made him uncomfortable, as though they were leveling an accusation that he wasn't a faithful Jew. Wasn't he going to Yerushalayim for Passover? Wasn't he one of the faithful, waiting and hoping for Messiah, who would come from the desert, east of the Holy City?

Yochanan often thought of that as he traveled this east-west wilderness road

---

5. Isaiah

to Yerushalayim. Someday the Messiah could be walking in this throng of pilgrims, along this very road. After all, Messiah would come not only from the east, but also from the wilderness. Certainly, there was no greater wilderness than the one Yochanan now faced as he headed for Yerushalayim. And hadn't the presence of God always entered the city from the east? God's people had entered Canaan from the east; God's ark of the covenant had entered the Temple from the east; and God's chosen king, Daveed,[6] had returned from the east to reclaim his throne after the death of his son Absalom.

The road from Yericho to Yerushalayim was uphill all the way, and for the first several miles, it was nothing more than a footpath winding around the sides of the barren Judean Mountains. On the right, so close that Yochanan didn't have to stretch out the full length of his arm to touch it, the mountain rose steeply overhead; he couldn't see the top. On the left, no more than a step or two away, the land dropped straight down into the canyon far below.

Though it was only a day's journey from Yericho to Yerushalayim, Yochanan always supplied himself with food and a full waterskin, especially during Passover season. At any time of year, this route was busy, but at Passover it became congested with travelers—most on foot, but some on donkeys and some pulling litters and other conveyances. In the narrowest spots, one person could not pass another without risking falling off the cliff. At those places, the old and infirm often blocked or slowed the way. Not being able to march along at his usual brisk pace annoyed Yochanan.

"You're in too much of a hurry," his friend Mikha'el[7] would say. "You're too impatient."

"'The sun rises and the sun sets, and hurries back to where it rises,'"[8] Yochanan would often reply, quoting one of the proverbs he always had on the tip of his tongue—though always with a smile for his best friend. "No time to waste."

Yochanan would see Mikha'el soon in Yerushalayim for Passover. In years past, they would have traveled together, but now that Mikha'el was married, he would be traveling with his wife, Elisheva,[9] and their families. Besides, Yochanan wanted to get there early to spend time with his rabbi.

"Yochanan!" a voice hailed him. He turned to see Gid'on,[10] a friend from Capernaum. It took a bit of maneuvering, waiting for a broader bit of path so

---

6. David
7. Michael
8. Ecclesiastes 1:5
9. Elizabeth
10. Gideon

they could let others pass, but soon the two men were able to walk together, one behind the other.

"So you've left your millstones for a time," Yochanan said. Gid'on and his family made some of the best millstones in Capernaum. Only a high holy day could take them from their profitable business.

"Yes," said Gid'on. "My family will come later in the week. I wanted to go early to hear some of the teachers of the Law, especially the rabbi from Natzeret,[11] the one called Yeshua.[12] But I've left my work for only a few days. Some of the fishermen from our town have abandoned their prosperous businesses altogether to become this teacher's talmidim[13]—Kefa[14] and his brother Andrew and the Zavdai[15] brothers."

"Many in Capernaum have followed him," Yochanan agreed.

"Including my sister Hadassah,"[16] said Gid'on. "I'm sure you know she suffered for years with an illness that made her unclean. Now she has been healed. She claims it was the new rabbi who did it. She believes he's the Messiah."

Yochanan nodded. "I've seen Hadassah at the synagogue," he said. "My mother told me she had been healed by the new teacher."

"I've just heard some interesting things about him in Yericho, too," said Gid'on.

"Like what?" asked Yochanan.

Apparently, according to what Gid'on had heard, the Galilean rabbi and his talmidim had been staying in the area for several days. During that time, Yeshua had healed a blind man and had had a much-talked-of encounter with the royal tax collector of the region, a man named Zakkai.[17] "He was a guest at the tax collector's house," said Gid'on.

"That must have caused quite a stir," Yochanan said. Devout Jews shunned the society of tax collectors, who were notorious for their immorality and dishonesty. Most of them got their positions by bribery and lived lavishly on the spoils of their trade. There were those who collected Herod's tax and the Temple tax, and these were tolerated. But many hated those who collected the emperor's

---

11. Nazareth
12. Jesus
13. (sing. talmid) A disciple or student of a rabbi whose desire was not only to know what his teacher knew but also to become like his teacher.
14. Peter
15. Zebedee
16. Esther
17. Zacchaeus

The Jericho Road. This narrow path in the Judean Wilderness follows the route of one of the ancient roads that led to Jerusalem from Jericho. Thousands of pilgrims traveled this and other routes during the three festivals of Passover, Shavuot, and Sukkot. (*Ray Vander Laan*)

tax. The Zealots in particular believed that since the emperor was considered divine by his subjects, paying tax to him was, in fact, idolatry.

"It did," said Gid'on. "But the most amazing thing was what Yeshua said to the man. His exact words, according to those who were nearby, were, 'Today yeshu'ah[18] has come to this house, because this man, too, is a son of Avraham.[19] For the Son of Man came to seek and to save what was lost.' "[20]

"What do you suppose he meant by 'save'?" asked Yochanan. "The Messiah will save us from the Romans. If he doesn't save us from the Romans, who is he going to save us from?"

"Perhaps this Yeshua is a new prophet," said Gid'on. "Or perhaps he means that Messiah will come this year."

Will Messiah come this year? Yochanan wondered, something he and every Jew

18. Salvation
19. Abraham
20. Luke 19:10

thought about each Passover. The priests even left the Temple door open, just in case Messiah arrived.

"Did you see Yeshua in Yericho?" asked Yochanan.

"No," said Gid'on. "I inquired about him but was told he had gone on to Yerushalayim for the feast. He—" Gid'on stopped abruptly. "Look!" He pointed ahead to a place where the path widened a bit. A rock slide partially blocked the way. "Someone has been injured."

The two men tried to hurry toward the spot but were slowed by pilgrims edging their way through the bottleneck, ignoring the man who lay in the road. Between the existing narrowness of the path and the rubble from the rock slide, the travelers had to step over the man to continue on their way.

"What happened?" Gid'on asked when they finally reached him.

"These rocks came down on me before I could get out of the way," said the man. "I think my leg is broken. Can you help me?" His dark eyes were glazed with pain. "While I was still stunned from the fall, someone grabbed my money pouch, so I fear I can't pay you."

The man was bleeding. If they touched him, they would be unclean for Passover. *That's probably why the pilgrims are ignoring him,* Yochanan thought. But they couldn't just leave him there, badly injured and at the mercy of anyone who passed by.

Looking back down the path, Yochanan saw a man on a donkey coming around the curve of the mountain. Standing with their backs flat against the mountainside so the other travelers could pass by, Yochanan and Gid'on waited for the man to reach them.

"This could make us unclean for Passover," Gid'on warned as they waited.

"I thought of that," said Yochanan with a nod. "But the man is injured."

They finally agreed they shouldn't let their religious duty get in the way of caring for this man in such need.

"Shalom!" said Yochanan as the man on the donkey drew near.

When the man returned their greeting, Yochanan realized from his accent that he was a Roman. For a moment, Yochanan was taken aback. Romans didn't travel the Yericho Road during Passover. It was the quickest way for them to get a knife in the ribs from one of the many Zealots among the pilgrims. And though the man was dressed modestly, the donkey indicated he was probably a person of means—another reason he shouldn't be here, at least not alone. There were many passes along the way where brigands could hide and waylay travelers, then escape again into the wilderness. The wilderness had been a place of escape for so many, good and bad.

The Roman didn't try to push past them, however, so Yochanan explained their predicament. "This man is injured and can't walk," he said. "I'll gladly pay you if you'll carry him on your donkey to the first wayside inn where he can get some help."

The Roman nodded and smiled. "I'm going as far as the fork to Yerushalayim. I can carry him to the inn there."

With so little room to maneuver, it was tricky work to get the man onto the animal, but soon the little caravan was on its way. Gid'on and Yochanan stayed with the Roman and the injured man until they reached the small inn. There he could get medical help and send a message to his family. When Yochanan tried to pay the Roman for his kindness, however, the man wouldn't hear of it and bid them a cheerful farewell.

Yochanan and Gid'on had been traveling for three or four hours now, and as they took the fork that led to Yerushalayim, the valley became broader and the pathway ran near the bottom of the wadi. Finding an indentation where the rocks made a natural bench, the two men stopped to eat their lunch of bread and cheese and the fresh figs Yochanan had purchased from the Yericho market. A tiny spring seeped from a crevice nearby, and they drank deeply from the fresh water, then refilled their waterskins.

From here, the road became flatter and wider, though it continued to climb. As the afternoon sun burned their shoulders, Yochanan and Gid'on approached the tops of the Judean hills, and the barren wilderness gradually gave way to rocky pastures divided by centuries-old stone walls. In many places, tall cypress trees lined the road. They passed small settlements and gently sloped hillsides dotted with flocks of sheep.

The closer they got to Yerushalayim, the more the excitement grew among the pilgrims mobbing the path. Children screamed with delight. Their parents exchanged shouts of shared celebration. Families sang and chanted the psalms of ascent.[21]

"I lift up my eyes to the hills. . . . My help comes from the LORD, the Maker of heaven and earth."

"He will not let your foot slip . . . he who watches over Israel will neither slumber nor sleep."

"If the LORD had not been on our side . . . the raging waters would have swept us away."

---

21. Psalms 120–134. These psalms were sung by the pilgrims as they climbed the road from Jericho up to Jerusalem.

The City of David. From the top of the Mount of Olives, the massive walls of Herod's Temple Mount are clearly seen. The Temple stood in the center where the Islamic Dome of the Rock now stands. On the left side of the Mount are the remains of the broad southern stairs where the pilgrims entered. Modern Jerusalem is just beyond. (*Ray Vander Laan*)

"The LORD has done great things for us, and we are filled with joy."

"Blessed are all who fear the LORD, who walk in his ways."

Many clapped their hands in delight and pointed when they saw the eastern slope of the Mount of Olives in the distance. The long mountain ridge with its clusters of villages grew closer and closer as they climbed higher and higher. They passed through the dusty main street of the village of Beit-Anyah,[22] then walked for a couple of miles along the crest of the mountain until they came to Beit-Pagey.[23]

Suddenly, as they came around the end of the mountain ridge and onto the western slope of the Mount of Olives, the moment arrived for which Yochanan and every other pilgrim had been waiting. There, 400 feet below, its walls and gates marching around Mount Zion, was Daveed's city, Yerushalayim. Nothing

22. Bethany
23. Bethphage

took Yochanan's breath away like that sight—not even the steepest grade on the Yericho Road—no matter how many times he saw it.

In the midst of the city, like a royal crown, stood the Temple built of purest white marble and gilded with sheets of gold. The long rays of the late afternoon sun struck brilliant sparks off the golden spikes that edged the top of the Temple, placed there to prevent birds from perching and soiling the sanctuary where God's presence, His Sh'khinah,[24] dwelled. Even the gates were golden—the gates that now would be open, waiting for the Messiah to arrive and take possession.

"Will Messiah come this year?" murmured Yochanan.

"Let us hope," said Gid'on. "This year in Yerushalayim!"

Jesus' road to the Cross started long before the Mount of Olives and the streets of Jerusalem. It started in Jericho, where He began His final journey to the Holy City. The ancient road from Jericho to Jerusalem, one of the most difficult in Judea, ascends, within a distance of 17 miles, from 800 feet below sea level to 2,500 feet above sea level. It goes from east to west, from the wilderness to the Holy City. By coming from the east, Jesus was announcing that He was the Messiah.

Six hundred years earlier, the prophet Isaiah had foretold, "In the desert prepare the way for the LORD; make straight in the wilderness a highway for our God" (Isaiah 40:3). By coming out of the wilderness, Jesus fulfilled that promise.

The prophet Ezekiel, 500 years earlier, had seen the glory of God depart from the Temple. As it did, it moved east, and the prophet had envisioned that glory, that presence, returning: "And I saw the glory of the God of Israel coming from the east. . . . The glory of the LORD entered the temple through the gate facing east" (Ezekiel 43:2,4). Jesus, who declared Himself to be God, came to the city for the last time—from the east.

Yet even as He walked to Jerusalem to fulfill and complete all His Father had promised, His sorrows had begun.

During the Passover season, thousands of pilgrims made their way to Jerusalem along the Jericho Road. (At one time, by Josephus's estimate, 3 million pilgrims filled the city for Passover.) Despite the crowds, however, the road was a desolate,

---

24. The glorious divine presence

lonely track through a barren wilderness. How much more so it must have been for our Savior! Ahead of Him were unimaginable suffering and death. Behind Him were His disciples—haggling over who would be first in the new kingdom.

Jesus' entire ministry had pointed toward His death on the Cross. His perfect life had been lived not simply to keep the Law, like the Pharisees, but also to show how to keep it fully. He had touched the lonely, the leper, the sick, the sinner, and the outcast, demonstrating daily to His disciples what they were to become. Their way was not one of violence, like the Zealots, but of service and self-sacrifice.

Yet those young men, Jesus' talmidim, who had spent three years with Him and dedicated themselves to becoming like Him, were now arguing about who was going to be the greatest among them. Imagine how that must have broken Jesus' heart! While He walked to an appointment with death, His closest friends, those with whom He would leave His ministry, were totally missing His message. All they cared about was asserting their need to rule and dominate in the new community.

The moment we begin to believe we must have power and authority—that we must be number one—to make a difference in the kingdom of God, that's the moment we lose sight of Jesus' life and sacrifice.

Jesus knew what lay ahead of Him, and He could have turned aside at any number of places along the way. Escape would have been simple. The Judean Mountains were pocked with countless caves, and all around Him was the wilderness, that place where Satan had tempted Him once before. In the blink of an eye, Jesus could have walked in a different direction.

But Jerusalem was waiting. Already the pilgrims were arriving, and the Temple priests were preparing for the week-long Passover feast. Already the sheep dealers from Bethlehem had their choicest animals in the market, and the people were picking their sacrificial lambs. One more year. One more sacrifice.

Jesus' willingness to walk the Jericho Road—His refusal to accept any other avenue except that which led to the Cross—is a measure of His devotion to God and His love for us.

Ultimately, that must become our measure and motive as well. As we walk through life, we can take only one path: the path of God's choosing, the path of obedience, the path to Christlikeness. Along the way, we may well find the kind of suffering and rejection that often accompany the life of a Christian living in this world, and we'll be tempted to turn aside and take a less difficult route.

But we must resist that temptation and stay on the path. Only then will we find the abundance of life Jesus offers.

Chapter 12

The Triumphal Entry

When it was almost time for the Jewish Passover, many went up from the country to Jerusalem for their ceremonial cleansing before the Passover. They kept looking for Jesus, and as they stood in the temple area they asked one another, "What do you think? Isn't he coming to the Feast at all?" But the chief priests and Pharisees had given orders that if anyone found out where Jesus was, he should report it so that they might arrest him. . . .

When he came near the place where the road goes down the Mount of Olives, the great crowd that had come for the Feast heard that Jesus was on his way to Jerusalem. They took palm branches and went out to meet him, shouting, "Hosanna!" "Blessed is he who comes in the name of the LORD!" "Blessed is the King of Israel!" "Blessed is the coming kingdom of our father David!" . . .

As he approached Jerusalem and saw the city, he wept over it and said, "If you, even you, had only known on this day what would bring you peace—but now it is hidden from your eyes. . . . you did not recognize the time of God's coming to you."

(John 11:55–57; Luke 19; Matthew 21; Mark 11)

Jerusalem, A.D. 30

Six days before Passover, the narrow streets were jammed with people. The smell of sweat and close-packed bodies competed with the sharp, acrid odor of blood. From every village and town, Jews were coming to Yerushalayim.[1] Filled beyond capacity, the city sent its overflow seeping into the surrounding towns and villages, as pilgrims found lodging wherever they could.

For many Jews, this Feast of Unleavened Bread celebrating their deliverance from bondage in Egypt and marking the beginning of the wheat harvest was bittersweet, surrounded as they were by the Roman presence. Tension in the city always ran high during the feast days, but Passover was especially volatile this year. As usual, extra troops had been ordered in from the Roman garrison at Caesarea, 45 miles west, on the Mediterranean coast.

Several factions anticipated or dreaded, depending on their perspective, the arrival of Yeshua,[2] the Natzrati[3] who had been proclaiming himself the Messiah. The man had been attracting followers in the Galilean countryside and even in the Decapolis, where crowds flocked to hear him preach in synagogues and on hillsides. Surely the Zealots would not pass up this opportunity to cause trouble. At least that's the way the Sadducees saw it. In fact, the Romans had already arrested several of the rebels, including one of the most vicious, the man named Bar-Abba.[4]

To make matters worse, a rumor was floating around that this Yeshua had raised some man from the dead over in the village of Beit-Anyah.[5] It seemed a ridiculous story, but those were the kinds of things that incited ignorant peasants and played into the hands of the Zealots.

---

1. Jerusalem
2. Jesus
3. (pl. Natzratim) Nazarene
4. Barabbas; *Bar* means "son of."
5. Bethany

E l'azar[6] was late for his meeting with Shim'on[7] and the other Zealots, but the road up from Yericho[8] had been crowded with pilgrims. Because of its narrowness, he could not move ahead of the families with small children and burdened donkeys. Then at one turn, a man had fallen on a rock slide that almost barricaded the road. That had held El'azar up for some time.

His sandals slapped on the paving stones as he crossed the Kidron Valley and hurried up the hill on the eastern side of the city. He shouldered his way through the Sheep Gate and the crowds in the marketplace beyond. If he weren't so late, he would have gone around to the northern Towers Gate.[9] The market near the sheep pool of Bethesda, close inside the Sheep Gate, was a mass of buyers and sellers as families, choosing their Passover lambs, bartered with dealers.

El'azar pushed his way through the shoulder-to-shoulder bodies into the equally crowded market streets. He hurried past the butchers, the cheesemakers, and the old women squatting on the paving stones with leeks, onions, and lettuces spread out around their feet like broad, green skirts. In the street of the bakers, the warm, comforting scent of fresh bread reminded El'azar that he had not eaten for hours. He bought two date cakes and washed them down with refreshing draughts from a wineskin he bought in the street of the winemakers.

His cousin Shim'on and the other men were already gathered at the home of Hevel,[10] who owned a small perfume shop in the city's lower quarter. They were at the back of the shop, closed for business, and as usual, they were arguing.

"This Yeshua is just another impostor," said one man, a boatbuilder from Caesarea who supplied them with news from the Roman stronghold. He knew little of the Galilean's notoriety and popularity. "We need to seize our own destiny, not wait for some mythical Messiah who is never coming."

"You don't know what you're talking about, Daveed,"[11] snapped Hevel, whose brother was even now imprisoned in the Antonia,[12] arrested for spitting at a Roman soldier. "This man is a born leader. People rally around him and hang on his every word."

"He's very clever," added Shim'on. "He maintains a low-key approach to the

---

6. Eleazar
7. Simon
8. Jericho
9. The Damascus Gate; the northern gate of Jerusalem.
10. Abel
11. David
12. The fortress built by Herod the Great immediately north of the Temple Mount and named after his friend Mark Antony. It was used by the Roman soldiers garrisoned in Jerusalem.

whole thing. But I believe, from a number of things he has said, that he intends to do something significant here during Passover."

"I agree," El'azar chimed in, and several others who had met Yeshua and heard him teach murmured assent. "This could be our golden moment—our deliverance and final victory over our oppressors."

"Pax romana!" Hevel said bitterly. "They achieve their peace at our expense!"

As they argued, their excitement grew, and plans were made. Even now, Shim'on said, Yeshua was on the other side of the Mount of Olives, preparing to enter the city. Many of his followers were already gathering in Beit-Anyah and along the road into the city. They needed to get out and rally them into a welcoming crowd.

"We need a sign of our resistance," said Shim'on.

"The palm branch," said Hevel. "We'll carry on the tradition of the Maccabees."

God had commanded palm branches to be waved on the Feast of Sukkot,[13] and ever since Y'hudah[14] Maccabee had reinstituted the feast after driving out the hated Greeks, the palm had become a symbol of Jewish freedom. The Sukkot prayer—the Hosannah—also had taken on an added, political dimension.

> O LORD, save us;
>   O LORD, grant us success.
>   Blessed is he who comes in the name of the LORD . . .
>   With boughs in hand, join in the festal procession
>   up to the horns of the altar.[15]

All agreed that the political symbol of their brave ancestors must be flaunted in the faces of their hated enemy. They could smell victory, and the scent was sweet indeed. Now they must go out and spread the word through the market-place and the local synagogues.

In the upper-city neighborhood, home of wealthy Jews and the politically astute Sadducees, the atmosphere was equally tense, especially among the group gathered in Nachum's[16] richly appointed living quarters. His lodgings were near the palace of the high priest Kayafa, who preferred to be called by his Greek name, Caiaphas. Several of the men paced the mosaic floor of the dining

---

13. Also known as the Feast of Tabernacles or Booths. It took place in late fall.
14. Judah
15. Psalm 118:25–27
16. Nahum

apartment, with its rich brown, cream, and terra-cotta patterns. The large wine cask in the corner would soon require replenishing.

"We can't have another incident," said one man whose aristocratic family had been influential in the powerful Temple hierarchy since the days of the Hasmonaean priesthood. "And I know Caiaphas is concerned about anything that might tip our balance of power and our image with Rome."

"I agree," said Nachum. "This Yeshua has amassed too many followers. Many of them are those Galileans—a bunch of fishermen and laborers. But the Zealots have been waiting for something like this, and they'll seize the opportunity if they can." He gestured for the servant standing by to refill the guests' wine cups, then sent him to the cellar for another jar.

"Fortunately, they caught Bar-Abba a few days ago," said one of the men, clenching his fists in anger. "I'm sure he and his gang killed my brother last year."

"The troops from Caesarea are already arriving," said another of the men, helping himself to dates and figs from a tray on the side table. "I thought maybe we'd get by without them this year, but you know Pilate. He knows what a hotbed this city becomes at Passover, and he'll leave nothing to chance."

These men didn't speak of Rome as an enemy or with bitter hatred. They were comfortable with the ruling power of Augustus Caesar, who allowed them to run the Temple as they pleased and wield their own power over the Jews. The Herods and the Pilates might come and go, but this Jewish priesthood and the court of the Sanhedrin really controlled day-to-day life and the economy in Yerushalayim and Judea. They wanted nothing to rock their boat.

Yet these men knew only too well the zeal of the patriots, the fire of their hatred, and the danger posed by so-called messiahs. Some of them still remembered Y'hudah from Gamla, who had stirred up a vicious revolt some years back. Though the man had been crucified, his family had been causing trouble ever since. The Sadducees hated and feared the Zealots. Not a few of them had felt the stealthy dagger or swift sword of these insurrectionists who killed real or imagined collaborators.

"We do have an informer," said Nachum, "a brother Judean. Some of you have met him. He's attached himself as one of Yeshua's inner circle, and he's contacted me from time to time. For the right price, I think we can have his cooperation in whatever we desire."

Stewing beneath the boiling cauldron of the city at Passover ran this undercurrent of opposition: the Zealots, who took any opportunity to provoke an incident, even as they waited and hoped for their political salvation to come from the east; and the Sadducees, sophisticated rulers of the Temple, who desired nothing more than the status quo and their own political and religious power.

Beyond the Sadducees' latticed windows, with their elaborately carved and inlaid cedar frames, much of the city was oblivious to these machinations and tensions, concerned only with the religious significance of the coming days. Pilgrims crowded the marketplace and the Temple, and the lamb dealers outside the Sheep Gate did a brisk business.

Rachel and her family had arrived from Beit-Lechem [17] with their flock several days earlier. For Passover, the Law required a lamb raised in Beit-Lechem, in the fields owned or controlled by the priestly class. Rachel's husband was pleased with the many perfect animals they had raised so carefully. The money earned during Passover week would keep them for the coming year.

Though Rachel was married, with children and grandchildren of her own, she still remembered that miraculous winter night all those years ago and the tiny baby she and the other shepherds had seen in the innkeeper's manger. She had often wondered what had happened to him. Perhaps he was somewhere in this city right now. Everyone came to Yerushalayim for Passover.

More likely, though, he was long dead. The spring sunshine warmed her shoulders, but she grew cold inside as she recalled the horror that had followed shortly after that midnight visit to the stable, when Herod had ordered all the boy babies in the town killed. Her baby brother had been one of the victims. Maybe that baby had been killed, too.

"Rachel!" her husband called. "Bring that lamb over there for this family."

Rachel drew her veil more closely across her face as she tugged the animal from the fold. Even as a child, she had never allowed herself to care about the gentle-faced creatures she tended, knowing their destiny. Yet something in their eyes caught her at times—a pleading resignation, perhaps? Some primitive understanding that their blood would be shed for a reason they could never comprehend? She led the lamb to the waiting family.

"Look, my son," said the father. "A lamb from Beit-Lechem. The very best."

As the lad reached out to pat the lamb's white mat of tight curls, Rachel wondered if the boy knew what all this was about.

She looked toward the south, where she could see the white and gold of the Temple rising above them. Was that really where God lived? When the priest stood in front of the burning incense and offered prayers for the people, and the

17. Bethlehem

people standing outside the Temple saw the smoke rising, was it really their prayers going up to God? When the priest sprinkled the blood on the goat and the goat was led into the wilderness to die, were they truly watching their sins being taken away? Certainly there was no escape for the scapegoat. Her father said the goat used to wander off, but now a person was chosen to lead the goat out and kill it. For as long as she could remember, she had wondered about this but had never dared to ask. It wasn't even a matter of seeming unfaithful. Women simply didn't talk about such things.

She should talk to Yochanah[18] about this. Her friend was so outspoken; surely she would not be offended. Yochanah was the one who had told her about the teacher from Galilee, the gentle rabbi who seemed to love and understand women as much as he did men. She wished she could see him, could sit at his feet the way Yochanah said some women did. When the men tried to send them away, the teacher had rebuked them.

Yochanah had tried to tell her many of the stories he told. Her favorite was the one about the good shepherd. She had also heard how he had calmed a storm and fed a large crowd with just a few loaves of bread and a few fish, and how a woman had been healed just by touching the tassels of his prayer shawl.

Suddenly, Rachel heard the crowds outside the Sheep Gate beginning to shout. "Look! He's coming! He's coming!"

"What are they shouting?" someone cried.

"It's the great Hosannah of Sukkot! They're pleading for God's deliverance."

Rachel glanced up fearfully at the Antonia. Soldiers lined the ramparts of the four towers. Would they attack the crowd? Why, on the day the lambs were chosen—the busiest day of the whole week of preparation—was this happening?

She threaded her way through the crowd and went out through the gate. She climbed onto a huge boulder near the city wall so she could see what was happening. A procession was coming down the Mount of Olives. On both sides of the path, people were shouting. Many of them were waving palm branches.

Rachel jumped down and moved up the path closer to the center of activity: a man on a donkey who had stopped the animal midway down the Mount of Olives. A group of travelers on foot, surrounding the man, also came to a halt, but the crowd continued to chant.

"Who is that man?" she asked a woman next to her, who was excitedly waving palm branches.

---

18. Joanna

"Yeshua," cried the woman. "Our deliverer."

The rabbi from Galilee! He was so close, Rachel could almost touch him.

"Is something wrong, Master?" one of the men with him said.

"What's going on?" asked another.

The rabbi didn't reply. He simply sat gazing at the white-stoned city spread out across the hills before them. White Yerushalayim stone gleaming golden in the spring sunlight. Beyond the Beautiful Gate rose the Temple Mount, level after level, ascending to God.

People jostled past Rachel, some glaring or yelling for her to get out of the way. But she stayed as close as she could to the teacher and the men around him.

The chanting grew louder and the waving palms more frenzied as the man nudged the donkey on its way again, down the steep hillside.

"Help, please, O Son of Daveed! Save us, please, O Son of Daveed!"

All eyes were on the man on the donkey, but his eyes were focused on the distance.

Rachel thought the teacher from Galilee would lead them directly through the Beautiful Gate into the Temple, away from the market with its mass of buyers and sellers. Instead, he turned onto the path that branched to the right, toward the Sheep Gate. The crowd surged behind him, and as the people closed in and the long, brittle leaves of the palms rattled around them, their chanting grew louder. "Blessed in the name of the LORD is he who comes! Save us, please, O Most High!"

Many spread their branches on the path before the donkey, and the people pressed closer and closer, some trying to touch the tassels on the rabbi's prayer shawl. "Help us! Save us! Hosannah! Hosannah!"

Rachel looked into Yeshua's face and was amazed. Tears had gathered in his dark eyes and were running down his cheeks into his tightly curled, black beard. His shoulders were shaking, as though he were sobbing. His talmidim,[19] pushed along by the crowd, struggled to stay protectively near him.

Suddenly, he began to speak, and Rachel could hear him, for those nearby grew silent and the shouts faded into the background. "If you, even you, had only known on this day what would bring you peace—but now it is hidden from your eyes," he said, weeping.

To whom was he speaking, the people around him or the city at which he gazed? Rachel couldn't tell, but she heard the agony in his voice as he shouted,

---

19. (sing. talmid) A disciple or student of a rabbi whose desire was not only to know what his teacher knew but also to become like him.

"The days will come upon you when your enemies will build an embankment against you and encircle you and hem you in on every side. They will dash you to the ground, you and the children within your walls. They will not leave one stone on another, because you did not recognize the time of God's coming to you."[20]

Everyone was looking for something on that Passover when Jesus was crucified. Religious Jews were looking for forgiveness from sin. Zealots were looking for the revolutionary who would lead them to freedom. Sadducees were looking for an incident-free week so that nothing would upset their balance of power. Rome's representatives were looking for crowd control. And every Jew was looking for the Messiah. Messianic fever always gripped the thousands of pilgrims thronging the streets of Jerusalem at Passover.

Then along came Jesus, a Jewish rabbi who had roused passionate devotion among His followers and intense hatred among His detractors. Who was this man, and why was He here?

The day Jesus entered the city of Jerusalem so triumphantly was the first day of Passover week. This was also the day Jews selected their sacrificial lambs. On that day, Jesus rode down the Mount of Olives from the east, the place from which the Jews knew the Messiah would come, saying, "Here I am, the Lamb of God, on My way to the throne by way of the Cross. Will you choose Me as your Lamb, as your sacrifice, and through that sacrifice, as your King?"

Many who greeted Jesus that day missed this point entirely. They were looking for a political leader—someone who would knock the weight of Roman rule from their backs. Waving the nationalistic symbol, the palm branch, they chanted political songs: "Hosannah to the one who comes in the name of the LORD! Hosannah to David!" Many were willing to make Jesus their Messiah, but only if He used the means they thought appropriate—military power. They were trying to make Jesus something He was not.

Accepting Jesus as one's King and Messiah means accepting Him for who He claimed to be. We can't remake Him into what we want Him to be. We can't keep the things we like and throw away the things we don't. If we want Jesus as the One who forgives our sins, we must also accept Him as the One who says, "Love

---

20. Luke 19:43–44

your enemies. Turn the other cheek. Pray for those who persecute you." If we want the Jesus who promises to relieve the burdens of life, we must also accept the Jesus who demands that we feed the hungry, clothe the naked, care for the poor and lonely, and visit the prisoner.

If we want the Jesus who, with power and conviction, confronts the evil of the demoniac and the hypocrisy of the religious leader, we must also accept the Jesus who touched the unclean and wept with the brokenhearted.

It's far too easy, however, even in our Christian community, to reshape Jesus into someone with whom we're comfortable.

The kingdom of Jesus comes through forgiveness, love, and witness, not through power and politics or any other worldly strategies. The kingdom of God comes as people accept, in their hearts, the Messiah for who He claimed to be.

Chapter 13

The Gethsemane

Each day Jesus was teaching at the temple, and each evening he went out to spend the night on the hill called the Mount of Olives.
(Luke 21:37)

Then Jesus went with his disciples to a place called Gethsemane. . . . Then he said to them, "My soul is overwhelmed with sorrow to the point of death. Stay here and keep watch with me."

Going a little farther, he fell with his face to the ground and prayed, "My Father, if it is possible, may this cup be taken from me. Yet not as I will, but as you will." . . . He went away a second time and prayed, "My Father, if it is not possible for this cup to be taken away unless I drink it, may your will be done." . . .

Then he returned to the disciples and said to them, ". . . Look, the hour is near, and the Son of Man is betrayed into the hands of sinners. Rise, let us go!"
(Matthew 26:36,38–39,42,45–46a)

Mount of Olives, A.D. 30

Silvery green olive leaves rustled in the breeze. Overhead, the azure sky was cloudless. Across the Kidron Valley, the golden walls of Yerushalayim[1] reflected the warmth of the morning sun, though here in the shade of the groves on the lower slopes of the Mount of Olives, the cool west wind, blowing in from the Mediterranean, still raised goose bumps on Mikha'el's[2] skin.

Something else was borne on the wind—the sounds of the city, alive with the joy of Passover. Wherever you went, you could hear the ceaseless noise. Here, it came as a great hum, like millions of bees.

Spring had arrived, a cause for rejoicing after the cold winter rains. Roadways and wadis would soon be dry and safe once more. The wet clay that sucked down everything that crossed it would soon give way to the dust of spring and summer. Even war often waited for the springtime.[3] Kings and armies dreaded having to march in winter, for their carts, chariots, and horses bogged down quickly in the thick, heavy clay of Judea.

On this second day of Passover week, pilgrims thronged the road that wound down the hillside of the Mount of Olives, across the valley, and up to the eastern city gates. Like a giant centipede, the crowds wriggled along, and mobs milled around the city gates.

At the bottom of the valley, the Kidron brook was dry, but the rocks were stained with the blood that drained down from the countless sacrifices being offered high above on the Temple altar. The wind carried the scent of burning flesh as the pilgrims gave their own offerings. An unending wave of sheep swept up the path that led to the Sheep Gate as the shepherds drove the animals to market.

Yesterday, when Mikha'el and his family arrived, the crowds had been even worse. At first, Mikha'el thought it was some political demonstration, for many

---

1. Jerusalem
2. Michael
3. 2 Samuel 11:1

of the people were yelling slogans, waving palm branches, and shouting the Hosannah: "Save us! Blessed is he who comes in the name of the LORD." That had startled him. The Feast of Sukkot[4] had been celebrated four months ago; the rainy season was past. What were these people praying for? What kind of deliverance? What kind of salvation did they want?

Then, in the midst of it all, he had recognized the famous rabbi from Galilee, riding on a donkey and surrounded by his talmidim.[5] Mikha'el knew several of them—fishermen from Capernaum.

Soldiers had been in evidence, too, watching the situation from the towers of the Antonia[6] just north of the Temple. Mikha'el expected them to slash into the crowd at any moment, swords swinging.

Though they hadn't, Mikha'el had wondered whether he had made the right decision about Elisheva.[7] Perhaps it had not been safe to bring her here. There was always political unrest in Yerushalayim, but it seemed to be increasing. Yet Elisheva had been insistent; she didn't want to miss Passover. A few months from now, it would be impossible for her to travel, for in six months' time she would deliver their first child. Mikha'el had been overjoyed when she told him the news. He was going to be a father! "We'll offer prayers and a sacrifice at the Temple," he promised her. He would ask the Lord for a safe birth and for a son.

Mikha'el and Elisheva had traveled here with their families. This morning, she and the other women had gone up to the city markets while the men visited the olive works of their friend Dani'el,[8] with whom they were staying in Beit-Pagey.[9] Though the village sat just on the eastern edge of the road that came around the ridge of the Mount of Olives, it was considered the city limits of Yerushalayim, being within a Shabbat's[10] walk.

Mikha'el had invited his friend Yochanan[11] to meet them there. Yochanan spent each day in the city with his rabbi, then returned to the cave of the sheepfold near Beit-Lechem.[12] Most rabbis came to Yerushalayim every day to debate

---

4. Also known as the Feast of Tabernacles or Booths. It took place in late fall.
5. (sing. talmid) A disciple or student of a rabbi whose desire was not only to know what his teacher knew but also to become like him.
6. The fortress built by Herod the Great immediately north of the Temple Mount and named after his friend Mark Antony. It was used by the Roman soldiers garrisoned in Jerusalem.
7. Elizabeth
8. Daniel
9. Bethphage
10. The Sabbath. It began at sundown on Friday night and ended at sundown on Saturday night.
11. John
12. Bethlehem

and teach, but they returned to any modest lodgings they could find at night. Today, however, Mikha'el had convinced his friend that Dani'el's olive operation was worth seeing.

Dani'el was a prosperous merchant who owned many of the groves on the western slope of the Mount of Olives. He also had a large home in Beit-Pagey, where he had made several rooms available to his friends and family during the feast days. Mikha'el's father had known Dani'el for years. Mutual business concerns had begun their acquaintance, which had, through the years, grown into a respectful friendship. For as long as Mikha'el had known Dani'el, the man had been wealthy. Only recently, however, had he also become generous.

Now the four men were strolling through the olive groves. Mikha'el never failed to marvel at the beauty of these trees, with their leaves that changed color with every breath of wind, from green to sparkling silver, and their wide, stalwart trunks. Because of their broad root system, olive trees had to be planted far apart. Dani'el was a wise man—he had filled the open spaces between the trees with grape vines.

During fall and winter, this place would be busy with workers harvesting the black olives and pressing out the oil at the gethsemane[13] in the nearby cave. Mikha'el could almost hear the voices and laughter of the men as they worked, the creak of wood against stone as the presses ground. And the smell! The air would be redolent with the pungent odor. No fragrance was more compelling than the fresh golden oil of olives. Like the smell of newly plowed fields, the scent saturated the countryside.

Placing the gethsemane in the huge, dry, warm cave in the Judean hillside was sensible. Warmth made the pressing easier, and the oil flowed more quickly. The first time Mikha'el had helped his father with pressing, when he was a boy of seven or eight, he had been amazed at how much oil ran out of the olives. When the enormous pressure of the limestone pillar bore down, the steady stream of oil ran golden, clear, and clean, without sediment.

The oil was almost sacred. For centuries, the Jewish people had used it to anoint kings, prophets, and priests. In Mikha'el's mind, olive oil and Passover were inextricably linked, for one day "the Anointed One" would appear at this season. Perhaps this year?

"Some of these trees must be hundreds of years old," Yochanan said just then.

"They are," said Dani'el. His dark eyes were bright with pride.

"Don't they get too old to produce?" asked Yochanan.

---

13. An oil press; from the Hebrew *gat-shemanim*, which means "press of oils."

The Gethsemane. The remains of this olive press, or "gethsemane," were found in Capernaum near the Sea of Galilee. The olives were crushed as the round millstone rolled over them in the stone trough. The olive pulp in baskets was placed under the huge pillar beyond and drained into the pit just in front of it. (*Ray Vander Laan*)

"No," said Mikha'el's father. "A good farmer, like Dani'el here"—he clasped his friend's shoulder—"prunes his trees regularly to keep the growth new and vital." He pointed to several trees that had been cut off at about eye level. "See the new growth springing from those stumps?"

"That's the amazing thing about the olive," said Dani'el. "When old trees are cut down, new shoots are born and soon become producing branches."

"So you get life out of that which appears dead," said Yochanan.

"That's my friend, the soon-to-be rabbi," Mikha'el said with a smile. "Always looking for the deeper meaning in everything."

"Don't you remember? 'A shoot will come up from the stump of Yishai;[14] from his roots a Branch will bear fruit,'"[15] replied Yochanan. "Those are words from Yesha'yahu[16] the prophet."

---

14. Jesse
15. Isaiah 11:1
16. Isaiah

"Ah, yes," said Dani'el. "A new shoot. A nezer. Just like Natzeret[17]—'the town of the shoot.' They chose that name because they think Messiah will come from them."

"As does every other town!" said Mikha'el. He touched some of the fresh, green shoots. The words Yochanan had spoken were familiar. His father had often said the stump of the olive tree was Israel. Israel worshiped idols, so it had to be cut down. *We are the new shoots,* his father would say. *And Messiah, when he comes, will be a shoot from Yishai's branch.*

They strolled a little farther—the two older men talking the business of olive pressing—until Dani'el gestured toward the mouth of a cave a few yards away. "My presses are in there, if you care to look," he said.

In the rocky cavern, the huge, rolling millstone—no doubt made in Capernaum—sat silent. Baskets used to gather the olives as they were picked, and more loosely woven baskets that later held the fruit as it was pressed, were piled in tall stacks in a natural alcove. The scent of season after season of pressing was strong here. A huge stone pillar and a heavy wooden beam rested full length on the rocky floor of the cave beside a vat stained with oil.

"How do you lift that enormous weight onto the olives?" asked Yochanan.

Dani'el pointed to a blunt hole cut into the rock above their heads and explained how that supported one end of the wooden beam. After the finest virgin oil had been crushed from the olives with the millstone, the remaining pulp was placed in baskets. These were stacked above a small vat—Dani'el pointed to the cavity cut into the rock floor of the cave—and topped with the huge stone pillar. Pressure was then applied by weights suspended from the wooden beam, anchored in the wall above. As the stone pressed down on the baskets of olive pulp, the oil ran through the baskets and into the stone vat below.

With Yochanan's curiosity satisfied, Dani'el led them to another alcove. This one had a wooden door with a lock on it. He took a large iron key from the pouch fastened to his belt and inserted it into the lock. The door opened onto a storeroom filled with tall jars. "This is my reserve," said Dani'el. He and Mikha'el's father began a cheerful argument about how much prices would rise over the spring and summer.

"A shrewd businessman always keeps a reserve," Mikha'el told Yochanan, nodding at the two. "Then, when oil becomes scarce, he can demand a higher price."

"You have quite an operation here, my friend," Mikha'el's father said. "I would like to see it during the pressing." He would not, of course. When harvest came,

---

17. Nazareth

he would be too busy with his own pressing operation in Capernaum.

As Dani'el closed and locked the door, Mikha'el noticed a few small bundles of goods and bed mats piled against one wall of the cave, and he wondered if some of the pilgrims had taken shelter there. People got premium prices during the feast days, renting out any space available, no matter how mean. Dani'el could get many shekels for a place like this, so convenient to the city.

The older man seemed to have read Mikha'el's thoughts, for he nodded toward the bundles and said, "The nights are still cool and the dew heavy, and this cave sits empty. I have offered the place to a Galilean teacher and his talmidim. They stay here at night." He waved his hand dismissively. "It's just my way to help the poor."

Dani'el didn't speak much about it, but he had once told Mikha'el that he'd had an encounter with the famous Galilean rabbi that had changed his life. He said he now knew what true obedience to the Law meant. It was the kind of thing people often said after they met the rabbi or heard him teach. Mikha'el wasn't sure what it meant, but it apparently had something to do with giving a great deal to the poor.

The men wandered out of the cave and down through the trees to the road. Once again, Mikha'el noticed the sound rising from the far hillside, where Yerushalayim shone golden in the sunlight. The majestic Temple reached toward the heavens.

That was one thing the Edomite, Herod the Great, had done well, Mikha'el thought, refurbishing the house of the Almighty and rebuilding its walls. Herod's intentions rang hollow, though, when he set the golden Roman eagle over the entrance to the Antonia, right next to the Temple. Some Pharisees had torn it down because it was an image, but after the leaders of the insurrection had been burned alive and their talmidim crucified for their offense, the blasphemous image had been promptly restored to its place. It was still there today, a constant source of pain and anger for the Jewish people.

Mikha'el thought again of the child his wife was carrying. Their son would be his inheritance from Jahweh, the blessing of the Almighty, one who would carry on his name and place. Like an olive tree, declared Yirmeyahu [18] the prophet.

> The Lord called you a thriving olive tree with fruit beautiful in form. [19]

---

18. Jeremiah
19. Jeremiah 11:16

Israel *was* God's olive tree. God planted and cared for Israel just as Mikha'el and his father and Dani'el planted and cared for their trees. And one day, his son would become one of those new shoots from the stump. His people had lost so much through the centuries. Yet . . .

> *"The days are coming," declares the* LORD,
>> *"when I will raise up to Daveed a righteous Branch,*
> *a King who will reign wisely*
>> *and do what is just and right in the land.*
> *In his days Y'hudah*[20] *will be saved*
>> *and Israel will live in safety.*
> *This is the name by which he will be called:*
>> *The* LORD *Our Righteousness."*[21]

"Come, Mikha'el," his father called. "Let's see if we can find the women before the crowds get any heavier."

Dani'el returned to his home in Beit-Pagey, while the other men set off across the valley floor and up through the eastern gate into the city.

D espite the closely pressed crowds, Mikha'el and his companions were able to catch up with the women, who were resting near the broad stairway along the southern wall of the temple.

Elisheva, her mother, and Mikha'el's mother had obviously enjoyed looking for bargains and haggling over goods at the shops and bazaars along Tyropean Street. Elisheva showed Mikha'el the fine cloth she had bought for their baby.

As they talked, the crowds pushed past them. The noise was almost deafening. Pilgrims drifted in and out of the city throughout the week of preparation, but toward the end, on the day of Passover itself, they swelled to overwhelming strength. It was said that the people of Yerushalayim numbered 80,000, but that during Passover the population swelled to more than a million, making it almost impossible at times to pass through the more popular areas around the Temple Mount.

"Mikha'el!" His mother's voice interrupted his thoughts, reaching him over the noisy hum. "You just missed all the excitement."

"Doesn't look like it to me," Mikha'el said with a laugh as he looked around at the congested stairways. A merchant ran down the southern stairs, chasing two

---

20. Judah
21. Jeremiah 23:5–6

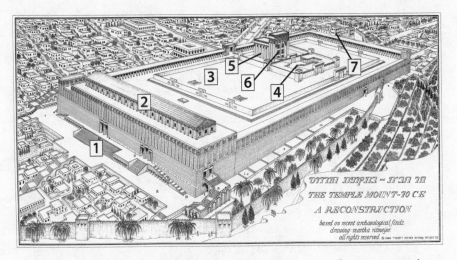

Herod's Temple Mount. The Temple courts and the Temple itself were magnificent structures without parallel in the ancient world. Each court was closer to the Temple itself, bringing the worshiper ever closer to the presence of God. (1) southern stairs; (2) royal stoa; (3) Court of the Gentiles; (4) women's court; (5) Temple; (6) priests' court and altar; (7) Antonia. (*Leen Ritmeyer*)

runaway goats. He was followed by a crowd of children, shrieking in delight. Several money changers rushed past, shekels[22] clutched in their hands and money pouches dangling from their belts. Clusters of people talked excitedly, gesturing toward the hallways that led from the stairway up to the Temple.

"The rabbi from Galilee just attacked the money changers in the Temple," his mother said. "Can you imagine?"

"And some shepherds are saying he turned their sheep loose," said Elisheva. "They're milling around all over the place."

"Sounds like a typical Passover to me," said Mikha'el.

Yerushalayim was always pandemonium at this time of year. On Passover alone, thousands of sheep had to be sacrificed. And that didn't even count the other days of sacrifice or the multitude of smaller thank offerings, such as the birds.

Challenging or opposing the buyers and sellers in the Temple complex was nothing new. Originally, the religious markets that sold incense, white robes, doves, pigeons, oil, and trinkets had been located in the royal stoa that ran along and above the southern Temple wall. Through the years, however, the number of sellers and their goods had increased so much that the Sadducees had expanded the market into the Court of the Gentiles.[23] This was extremely offen-

---

22. A coin used to pay the Temple tax.
23. The place where Gentiles were allowed to gather and pray by the Temple in Jerusalem.

sive to the Essenes and others who felt the priesthood had become increasingly materialistic, wealthy, and aristocratic.

Twenty years earlier, an Essene had driven thousands of sheep through the area, completely disrupting the market, and then had begun shouting words from Yesha'yahu the prophet:

> *Foreigners who bind themselves to the Lord*
> > *to serve him,*
> *to love the name of the Lord,*
> > *and to worship him . . .*
> > *and who hold fast to my covenant—*
> *these I will bring to my holy mountain*
> > *and give them joy in my house of prayer.*
> *Their burnt offerings and sacrifices*
> > *will be accepted on my altar;*
> *for my house will be called*
> > *a house of prayer for all nations.* [24]

The offense was against the Gentiles, for the Sadducees had put the sheep market where the Gentiles came to worship. Since Gentiles couldn't enter any of the other courts, by doing this, the priests had usurped their place of prayer. God had commanded that faithful Gentiles needed a place to pray, but the Sadducees had decided that on religious days they needed a market more.

"What did the Galilean say when he did this?" asked Yochanan.

"He shouted, 'It is written, "My house will be called a house of prayer," but you are making it a "den of robbers"!'" [25]

"Well, he's right," said Yochanan. "With the market there, the Gentiles have no place to pray. Is this the rabbi we've heard at the synagogue in Capernaum?"

"Yes," said Elisheva.

"I'm not surprised then," said Mikha'el. "From what I've seen and heard, he's bold and fearless."

"Come on," said Yochanan. "Let's see if he's still here. Maybe he's teaching somewhere in the Temple."

Everywhere we go, Mikha'el thought as they pressed through the crowds, *we seem to encounter the Galilean rabbi.* What else was the man going to do this week? Could anything more happen? Dani'el had said the teacher and his

---

24. Isaiah 56:6–7
25. Matthew 21:13

students were staying at the gethsemane every night. *Perhaps on our way back to Beit-Pagey, I'll stop and see if he's there*, Mikha'el thought.

During the last week of His life, as He prepared to offer Himself as the final sacrifice for sin, Jesus taught every day in the Temple and spent every night on the same hillside where He'd begun the week in triumph. The first day of Passover, He had traveled down the road from Bethany to Jerusalem, where He was hailed as the answer to the Jewish people's prayers. He was, the crowds shouted, the one who would enable them to triumph over their earthly enemies.

At that time, this western slope of the Mount of Olives was thick with fertile olive groves, and oil presses (gethsemanes) would probably have been nearby. In fact, the remains of an olive press were discovered in one of the large caves there.

Somehow, it wouldn't be surprising if Jesus had chosen a place like that to spend His last week and night on earth. The quiet darkness of the olive grove and the isolation of the cave, away from the city crowds, would have been appealing. In fact, this gethsemane could be seen as a powerful metaphor and messianic symbol for what He would ultimately do.

The precious oil obtained from the olive had a variety of uses. One was the anointing of prophets, priests, and kings. To be anointed meant that a person was recognized and equipped to carry out a specific responsibility before God. *Messiah* is the English word for the Hebrew *Moshiach*, meaning "anointed." Thus, the ultimate Anointed One of God is the Messiah. The olive and its oil, then, are related to the promise of God's Anointed, His Messiah, Jesus.

After they were harvested, the olives were placed under the weight of a heavy stone pillar. The enormous pressure of that gethsemane squeezed the precious oil out of the olives.

On the night of His betrayal and arrest, Jesus went to the olive grove. As He crossed the Kidron Valley, red with the blood of sacrifices from the Temple above, He faced the enormity of what He was about to do, what it meant to be God's Anointed. His blood would be the fulfillment for countless sacrifices for hundreds of years—and for numberless generations to come.

Even as thousands of pilgrims were presenting their sacrifices, even as the high priest prepared to offer up the yearly sacrifice for the sins of the people,

Jesus was about to become the Passover sacrifice, the Lamb whose blood would be shed for the sins of the world.

In doing this, He faced the ultimate rejection of His own people. Even His closest friends, His talmidim—those who were supposed to become like Him— would deny Him. And He knew it. Worst of all, He would be rejected by His heavenly Father, God Himself.

As Jesus bore the weight of what it meant to be the Lamb of God and the sacrifice for the sins of the world, drops of His anointing blood began to seep from Him, like precious oil being squeezed from olives. Jesus willingly placed Himself under such agony to show us the intensity of His love. Our need drove Him there and placed Him under the incredible gethsemane of His sacrificial death.

Jesus' gethsemane is our gethsemane. Because He was pressed out for us, we will never have to bear the weight of the penalty for our own sins.

Chapter 14

The Final Sacrifice

And they crucified him. Dividing up his clothes, they cast lots to see what each would get.
It was the third hour when they crucified him.

(Mark 15:24–25)

From the sixth hour until the ninth hour darkness came over all the land. About the ninth hour Jesus cried out in a loud voice, "Eloi, Eloi, lama sabachthani?"—which means, "My God, my God, why have you forsaken me?"

(Matthew 27:45–46)

Jerusalem, A.D. 30

His boots slapped against the stones as Marcus hurried through the city. Trying to find his way in the maze of winding streets that climbed up and down hills and into dead-end alleyways aggravated his frustration. Being packed with thousands of loud religious Jews made the streets even worse. Even at daybreak they were busy, with markets and shops preparing to open. The smell of raw meat, freshly slaughtered, mingled with the earthy odor of vegetables and the fragrance of baking bread. The latter was tempting, but he wanted nothing more than to get out of this congestion and noise. He'd never known a people who talked so much or so loudly, jabbing their fingers and leaning into each others' faces.

Though Yerushalayim[1] was usually patrolled by the tenth legion, the procurator in Caesarea had called for additional troops from the fifteenth. Pilate himself had left the shores of Caesarea and was in residence at the Antonia,[2] hoping his presence would keep the restless Jews in order. Herod Antipas was in the city for the same reason. Then again, it could be just another power struggle between those two rumored enemies.

As far as Marcus was concerned, he'd rather be in Caesarea, with its cool Mediterranean breezes—or back in the rolling, green hills of the Galilean countryside and the sophisticated cities of the Decapolis. Being ordered away had not pleased him. Not that things were easy there. With the Zealots increasing their terrorist tactics—burning villages and poisoning wells—keeping the peace was never simple. But he was a soldier, and that's what he was paid to do. This crowded city, with its constantly bubbling cauldron of political and religious unrest, was another matter.

Gaius was here, too, and he was no happier. They'd been in Yerushalayim

---

1. Jerusalem
2. The fortress built by Herod the Great immediately north of the Temple Mount and named after his friend Mark Antony. It was used by the Roman soldiers garrisoned in Jerusalem.

only a few days when they'd been ordered to crush a possible riot. The city was filled with Zealots, always looking to make trouble. But that day even the ordinary citizens seemed out of control, waving palm branches and shaking their fists in Rome's face. The scene had gotten so tense that Marcus was sure his centurion would order wholesale slaughter. Gradually, things had calmed down without bloodshed, although an underlying tension still gripped the city—as though something were seething and sooner or later would boil over.

Marcus plunged out of the early-morning shadows of the narrow residential street into the outer court of the Antonia, the fortress named after Mark Antony, one of Herod the Great's patrons. He walked across the pavement and entered the inner courtyard, which was surrounded by soldiers' quarters. This was the place the men gathered when they weren't on duty in the city or on the watchtowers above.

In one corner, beside a fire built to take off the morning chill, a group of bored off-duty guards knelt on the huge rectangular stones, playing basilikos.[3] As they took turns throwing the dice across the game board permanently scratched into the rock, they drank wine and laughed. Basilikos was a favorite of the troops, and they would gamble for just about anything.

Just then he heard hooves on stone, and a horse and rider clattered through the archway and into the courtyard.

"Marcus," hailed Gaius, reining in his mount. He unhooked his chin strap, pulled off his helmet, and ran his hand through his sweat-dampened hair. He swung himself from the saddle. The horse stamped and snorted as Gaius turned the reins over to a stable servant, who led the animal away. "Where did you disappear to?"

"Just as we were ready to move out, I was ordered to see about a knifing in the lower city," Marcus said with a laugh. "I can't believe the way these Jews kill each other. The only thing they seem to agree on is that they hate us!"

"Where's your prisoner?" asked Gaius.

"The culprit was long gone. You can hide anything in this maze of streets." He noticed Gaius's sweat-stained tunic. "Did you execute them yet?"

"No. The squad is out there now, and the poor wretches are on their way, carrying their crossbeams." Gaius shrugged his wide shoulders several times, as though relieving tension. "The poles are all in place."

---

3. Means "the game of the king"; a game played with dice. One of the playing boards for this game can still be seen in Jerusalem, scratched into a huge paving stone.

"This was certainly a hurried affair," said Marcus. "But I've been expecting something all week, as high as tensions have been running. Did we finally catch more of the ring leaders, or is Pilate just getting rid of Bar-Abba?"[4]

"Haven't you heard?" said Gaius. "Pilate let Bar-Abba go."

"That's not possible. He's a murderer! He's the worst of the Zealots. After all the months we've been after him—and the high priest screaming for us to get him—why would Pilate release him?"

"Pilate offered a deal, and the priests traded him for the Galilean who was causing all the ruckus the other day. He's the same one the crowd was waving palm branches for a few days ago."

Marcus still couldn't believe what he was hearing. "Bar-Abba has knifed as many Sadducees as he has Romans. If they let him go in exchange for the Galilean, they must really hate the man," he said.

"Apparently, someone turned him in late last night," said Gaius, "and before dawn the Sadducees were demanding that Pilate execute him."

"So that's what all the hubbub was about this morning! I noticed a lot of people around when I moved out before dawn. That must have made the old boy happy," Marcus said with a grin. "He loves demands."

"Yes," sneered Gaius. "He probably would have ignored them, but I guess the Temple powers want this man dead—and fast. It was all very secretive. They didn't want the rest of the Jews to know about it. The charges sound trumped up to me, but for some reason, Pilate complied."

"You'd think these Jewish rebels would learn, wouldn't you?"

"You'd think so," said Gaius. "Peaceful coexistence seems a small price to pay to avoid hanging on a cross."

The voices of the soldiers playing dice in the corner suddenly rose in a squabble. Somebody had cheated.

"We'd better go back out and get this over with," Gaius said, shoving his helmet on his head.

Marcus groaned inwardly at the thought of what lay ahead. Though many of his compatriots delighted in the brutality, Marcus hated crucifixion. He was a legionary, not a barbarian, and except for the worst of felons, the agony of the torturous death seemed extreme. The few times he had witnessed mass crucifixions or been detailed to a death squad, the scene had stayed with him for weeks.

---

4. Barabbas; *Bar* means "son of."

The Sixth Hour

Yochanah[5] fingered the heavy, woolen material. It would make a warm and beautiful mantle. The wool merchant carried only the best cloth and thread, but all of it was costly, and she had no extra money. Before leaving Galilee, she had given Yeshua[6] and his talmidim[7] as much of her household funds as she could afford. She had been hoarding every extra shekel[8] she could manage. Knowing the expenses the rabbi and his talmidim would have during the feast of Passover in Yerushalayim, she and her friends had wanted to help them as much as possible.

Her husband, Cuza, had not come to Yerushalayim with Herod this time but had stayed at the palace at Tiberias to oversee the building projects. Herod planned to be here only a short time anyway—just long enough to make sure there was no trouble during Passover and to keep ahead of the Romans. Besides, with his views, Cuza would be in danger here. Their Zealot countrymen considered pro-Roman Jews traitors and readily slid a knife between their ribs—anytime, anywhere.

Cuza had not been particularly happy that Yochanah had left the household at this time either, but she insisted on making the pilgrimage for Passover. Also, she sensed she needed to be near the Galilean rabbi from whom she had learned so much. His teaching had become increasingly intense over the last few weeks, and many of his followers had left him because of some startling things he'd been saying. As she listened to him, something had clenched inside her, as though some portentous thing was about to happen. Cuza, who had no faith except in his own abilities and Herod's power, would have laughed at her had she confided her feelings, but her womanly instinct had been right too many times to ignore it.

Though the wool shop was busy and crowded, it was still a respite from the streets, thronged with pilgrims. Once she got out in that endless wave of bodies, she would be swept along.

She stroked the material longingly, then turned away. Maybe next time. She wrapped her shawl about her and pulled it over her head as she pushed out of the small shop and into the wide Tyropean thoroughfare along the valley floor below the western Temple wall.

---

5. Joanna
6. Jesus
7. (sing. talmid) A disciple or student of a rabbi whose desire was not only to know what his teacher knew but also to become like him.
8. A coin used to pay the Temple tax.

Despite the hour and the season, the air was cool. Yochanah looked up. The sun should have been high; it was midday. Instead, the atmosphere seemed strangely shadowed. It didn't feel like rain, yet clouds were racing in, obscuring the sun, gray and growing darker. Added to this, she could feel tremors shaking the ground. Though they weren't uncommon, they were always disconcerting.

She turned north on Tyropean Street and walked toward the market streets in the city. Last night she had stayed with Herod's household in the Hasmonaean palace, and she'd had a restless night. She'd been awakened in the early hours by shouting. One of the slaves said a prisoner had been brought in. That must have made Herod happy. He hated getting up in the middle of the night.

Tonight, however, she wasn't returning to the palace. She would be sharing a room with several women near the Essene quarter in the upper city. They were planning to celebrate tomorrow's Feast of Unleavened Bread with some of Yeshua's disciples. Shabbat[9] began at sundown tonight, so she needed to lay in supplies, since she was helping to provide and prepare the meal.

As she entered the street of the bakers, people pressed against her on all sides. She kept her right hand tightly clasped on the small coin pouch tied beneath her sash, trying to plant her sandals firmly at each step to keep from slipping. The noise was deafening, and everything was a blur.

Working her way out of the middle of the street toward the left-hand side of the passage, Yochanah felt sharp elbows against her ribs and dull heels and toes kicking her shins and calves. Finally, she made it into the bakery she wanted, a cavelike room beneath the houses overhead. Women shouted and haggled over the price of bread, and the fresh, moist smell almost made her sick to her stomach. She hadn't realized she was so hungry. She bought her loaves and continued into the heart of the marketplace, pinching off a piece of bread as she walked. She was starting to swallow the first bite when the bread suddenly stuck in her throat. Her sickness was no longer from hunger.

Coming down the steep street from the Towers Gate,[10] shoving their way through the crowd, came a squad of Roman soldiers. She heard the hisses as men and women huddled and whispered at the side, watching them pass.

The brutal, tanned faces beneath the helmets came closer, and she caught the eyes of the one nearest to her. Eyes of a Roman—blue, piercing, and cold. Yet he wasn't talking or laughing as several of the others were. One soldier, his forearms

---

9. The Sabbath. It began at sundown on Friday night and ended at sundown on Saturday night.
10. The Damascus Gate; the northern gate of Jerusalem.

spattered with blood, carried a hammer, and a bag clanked against his hip. Iron spikes. The brutal sight sickened Yochanah.

Suddenly, she heard words that sent chills down her spine.

"Did you notice the charge posted above the Galilean rabbi?" scoffed one soldier. "King of the Jews? What a joke!"

Yochanah clasped the bread tightly against her breast and watched the soldiers' broad, leather-covered backs fade into the crowd. The reference to a Galilean could mean anything, of course. There were many Zealots from that area, and many had been executed. But a rabbi?

Which way to turn? Who to ask?

She couldn't bear the thought of going to the place outside the city gates where the Romans carried out their atrocities, but she had to know. Taking a street off to the right, she made her way toward the northern city gate, looking for a familiar face, someone to reassure her.

The fear in the woman's dark eyes had chilled Marcus's heart and pierced his soul—as though she could see into his mind . . . see the sights still captured there. The smell of blood and fear filled his nostrils. The sounds echoed in his head—iron smashing bone, screams of pain fading to ghastly, gasping struggles to breathe against the agony and slow death.

Overhead, one thin band of gray streaked the ink-stained sky. Marcus crossed the Antonia courtyard, heading for his quarters. The ground was firm once more; the shaking from the earthquake had passed. But he still felt unsteady. Somehow, it felt like the end of the world.

The men had still been alive on their crosses when he left, and he couldn't get the middle one out of his mind. Gaius was right. Why had they crucified that man? And his crime had been written on the posting over his head: King of the Jews. That didn't even make sense.

"Marcus, join the game!" shouted one of the men gathered around the basilikos gaming stone. "We're playing for the 'king's' tunic."

"No thanks," he said. He looked around for Gaius but didn't see him. Perhaps he was still on the hill.

The sights and words he had heard kept running through his mind. Some of the leading priests and Sadducees had been screaming for the man's blood. But how could Pilate even have listened to them? They said the man had claimed he could destroy the Temple and rebuild it in three days. That might make him a candidate for lunacy, but certainly not death. That charge would never stand in a Roman court of law.

Fear leads people to do terrible things, Marcus thought. How could one man's ideas stir such tremendous hatred? What kind of threat did he pose? It had to be something like that to make them want to get rid of him so badly.

Who was this man?

The Ninth Hour

Yochanah huddled with the other women near the high city wall outside the gate. She couldn't bring herself to go any closer to the hill where the three men hung.

Yeshua crucified. Was this the terrible thing that had haunted her for the past weeks—the strange foreboding she had felt?

Suddenly, in the distance, she heard the sound of the shofar, from high on the southwestern corner of the Temple Mount. As the hollow notes echoed across the city, the din behind the walls seemed to diminish.

It was the ninth hour. Time for the final sacrifice of Passover.

Then, out of the silence, she heard a shout from the crosses. "It is finished!"

Every day for more than a millennium, since the time of Moses, the priests had offered sacrifices for the sins of God's people at the third hour and the ninth hour—at dawn and at three in the afternoon. And each year since the time of Moses, Israel had celebrated Passover, and the priests had offered the daily sacrifice at three on the afternoon before Shabbat and the Feast of Unleavened Bread.

Now all those offerings came to one great, final conclusion as God's Lamb, presented to the people as He rode into Jerusalem on lamb-selection day, was offered at the exact hour of the last sacrifice on Passover. More than 1,200 years of sacrificial offerings—all pointing to the one great sacrifice of God. What care and planning God put into His great work of redemption!

Nearly two millennia before, God had appeared to His nomad friend Abraham. In the midst of promises of land, descendants, and a mysterious blessing for all nations, God and Abraham created a path of blood through which Almighty God passed, staking His life on the fulfillment of His promises.

Now, hanging on a cross outside Jerusalem—His blood dripping onto the same soil on which the blood path between Abraham and God had been formed—the Son kept His Father's word. Nothing, not even the sinfulness of Abraham and his descendants, could stand in the way of the fulfillment of that promise—even if it meant that God paid the price with His own blood.

Each fall on Yom Kippur, the great day of atonement, the high priest of the Temple symbolically transferred Israel's sins onto the head of a goat. This animal was then led outside the city walls and into the wilderness to die, thereby removing the sins of the people from their community. Jewish tradition says that to prevent the goat from wandering back, as it would naturally do, the priests commissioned someone—not an Israelite—to wait in the wilderness and kill it.

Now Jesus, God's scapegoat, was taken outside the city to die. When the Son of God reached the appointed place, carrying the sins of the world on His shoulders, the Romans completed the awful task of execution.

There, hanging on a cross, the Son of God faced the ultimate rejection: "My God, My God, why have You left Me all alone?" And thus it was finished. At the moment the lamb was killed in the Temple, Jesus died on the cross, His work completed. The need for sacrifices had ended.

Jesus became both our lamb and our scapegoat. He carried our sins outside the camp, and He died for us, once and for all.

Chapter 15

The Feast of Pentecost

And when Jesus had cried out again in a loud voice, he gave up his spirit.

At that moment the curtain of the temple was torn in two from top to bottom.

(Matthew 27:50–51)

And the curtain of the temple was torn in two.

(Luke 23:45b)

While he was blessing them, he left them and was taken up into heaven. Then they worshiped him and returned to Jerusalem with great joy. And they stayed continually at the temple, praising God.

(Luke 24:51–53)

From the day after the [Passover] Sabbath, the day you brought the sheaf of the wave offering, count off seven full weeks.

Count off fifty days up to the day after the seventh Sabbath, and then present an offering of new grain to the LORD. . . . On that same day you are to proclaim a sacred assembly and do no regular work.

(Leviticus 23:15–16,21)

When the day of Pentecost came, they were all together in one place. Suddenly a sound like the blowing of a violent wind came from heaven and filled the whole house where they were sitting. They saw what seemed to be tongues of fire that separated and came to rest on each of them. All of them were filled with the Holy Spirit.

(Acts 2:1–4)

The Southern Staircase of the Temple, A.D. 30

I t was like a ripple in time that only a few noticed. More than two months had passed since the rabbi from Galilee had been executed by the Romans, and here they were again, in Yerushalayim[1] for another feast day. Nothing had changed. Everything had changed.

Once more, the broad southern staircase of the Temple was crowded with pilgrims. Once more, faithful Jews from every land had come to pray and sacrifice. This time it was for the Feast of Shavuot,[2] and they were bringing their harvest gifts of thanksgiving, just as Jahweh had commanded back in the days of Moshe.[3]

> When you have entered the land the Lord your God is giving you as an inheritance and have taken possession of it and settled in it, take some of the firstfruits of all that you produce from the soil of the land the Lord your God is giving you and put them in a basket. Then go to the place the Lord your God will choose as a dwelling place for his Name. . . . The priest shall take the basket from your hands and set it down in front of the altar of the Lord your God. . . . Place the basket before the Lord your God and bow down before him.[4]

The Jewish people had known Jahweh's presence for thousands of years. He walked with Avraham[5] in the Negev and met Moshe on Sinai. He parted the waters as Israel escaped from Egypt and crossed into Canaan. He guided them with pillars of fire and smoke and dwelled among them in the tabernacle and the ark. He brought them back from captivity in Babylon and lived once more in the

---

1. Jerusalem
2. Means "weeks"; also known as Pentecost or the Feast of Weeks. It's celebrated 50 days after the Sabbath following Passover.
3. Moses
4. Deuteronomy 26:1–10
5. Abraham

The Huldah Gates. The southern end of the Temple Mount was over 900 feet long. Above was the magnificent royal stoa. The large staircase, sometimes called the southern stairs, led to one double gate (for pilgrims) on the left, through which pilgrims entered to reach the Temple courts above. Between the two stairs were the ritual baths in which the pilgrims were purified before entering the sacred courts. (*Eyal Bartov*)

Holy of Holies. And His presence, Ruach HaKodesh,[6] the holy wind of God, was with them still.

Now, however, there were echoes of another presence.

Although the Romans had crucified Yeshua,[7] the popular young teacher from Galilee, more than 50 days ago, his disciples claimed he was alive again. He had risen from the grave!

These talmidim[8] had been staying in a home in the Essene quarter of the upper city, provided by one of Yeshua's wealthy followers, and each day they could be found at the Temple, praying and talking about him and his teachings. Then, on the holiest day of Shavuot, the disciples went together to the Temple with great excitement, as every Jewish believer was doing.

---

6. The Holy Spirit
7. Jesus
8. (sing. talmid) A disciple or student of a rabbi whose desire was not only to know what his teacher knew but also to become like him.

The courts and southern stairway were jammed with people trying to get into the Temple for the nine o'clock sacrifice, waiting in line as those ahead of them pushed and squeezed into every available space. Suddenly, the ground began to shake, then the building itself, and the sound of a great wind swept over them. They hung on to each other to keep from falling and looked up fearfully at the Temple walls, hoping they wouldn't collapse and crush them. Then, as quickly as it had begun, the trembling passed and the wind died away.

The crowd was breathing a sigh of relief and edging once more up the stairs when Yeshua's talmidim began shouting. It was as if they had suddenly gone out of their minds, for they weren't speaking in the language of the Temple. The disciples were all talking at once, and yet all the people—gathered from many nations—heard what they were saying in their own language.

Murmuring and muttering swept through the crowd. "What's wrong with these men? Have they gone mad?"

A man near the bottom of the stairs began to laugh. "They're drunk!" he shouted.

"We are not drunk!" yelled the disciple named Kefa.[9] "It's nine o'clock in the morning."

Then, surrounded by the other talmidim, he began shouting to the pilgrims gathered there: "Men of Israel, listen to this: Yeshua of Natzeret[10] was a man accredited by God to you by miracles, wonders, and signs, which Jahweh did among you through him, as you yourselves know."

He swept his arms out to his sides, as though encompassing all of them. "This man was handed over to you by Jahweh's set purpose and foreknowledge; and you, with the help of wicked men, put him to death by nailing him to the cross.

"But Jahweh raised him from the dead, freeing him from the agony of death, because it was impossible for death to keep its hold on him."[11]

With passion and eloquence, the fisherman-turned-talmid—a fiery young man reputed to have defended the Galilean with a sword and then to have denied knowing him—spoke of Jahweh's promised deliverer and how Yeshua had fulfilled that promise, even as the prophets had foretold.

"Jahweh has raised this Yeshua to life," Kefa said, "and we are all witnesses of the fact. Exalted to the right hand of Jahweh, he has received from the Father the promised Ruach HaKodesh and has poured out what you now see and hear. . . ."

---

9. Peter
10. Nazareth
11. Acts 2:22–24

"Therefore let all Israel be assured of this: Jahweh has made this Yeshua, whom you crucified, both Lord and Messiah."[12]

The veil had been torn, and the Spirit of God had moved out of the Temple and into the hearts and lives of His people.

Yochanan[13]

"**R**epent and be baptized, every one of you, in the name of Yeshua the Messiah for the forgiveness of your sins," Yeshua's disciple had said, "and you will receive the gift of the Ruach HaKodesh."

If Yeshua can forgive sins, does that mean no more sacrifices? Yochanan wondered. From the Temple steps, he looked toward the Kidron Valley. Even now the bottom would be red with the sacrificial blood of sheep and goats. Were these offerings no longer necessary?

He remembered the journey he and his rabbi had made to Arad three years ago and the blood-path covenant they had observed. Jahweh had promised that if Israel did not keep the covenant He had made with Avraham, He would give His life. As faithful as Yochanan and many of his fellow Jews tried to be, he knew their people had not always been obedient.

Had the Almighty given His own life?

Yes, Yochanan thought, *I believe He has. Maybe Yeshua really is the final sacrifice.*

Mikha'el[14]

Our *son will be born soon,* Mikha'el thought. He was standing with the rest of the people outside the Temple in Yerushalayim, waiting to celebrate the Feast of Shavuot. Because her time of delivery was close enough to make travel uncomfortable, Elisheva[15] had not accompanied him, but she had made him promise to bring word of the Galilean rabbi. Many in Korazin and Capernaum had been grieved by word of his death, and they had learned few details of the event or why the Romans had crucified him.

Mikha'el thought of that night during Passover week when he had returned alone to Dani'el's[16] gethsemane[17] and found Yeshua and his talmidim in the cave. There, he had been mesmerized by the Galilean's words.

---

12. Acts 2:32–36
13. John
14. Michael
15. Elizabeth
16. Daniel
17. An oil press; from the Hebrew *gat-shemanim*, which means "press of oils."

God's Olive Tree. This olive tree represents God's people throughout history. The ancient trunk and roots are Israel (note the faces of Abraham and Sarah). The branches are the people who follow the Messiah (note the people that make up the leaves). Non-Jews were grafted in as branches to God's tree of Israel (Romans 11:17). (*Elmer Yazzie*)

"I am the true vine," Yeshua had said, "and my Father is the gardener. He cuts off every branch in me that bears no fruit, while every branch that does bear fruit He prunes so that it will be even more fruitful."

God's olive tree, Mikha'el had thought. *We are God's olive tree.*

"I am the vine," repeated Yeshua. "You are the branches. If a man remains in me and I in him, he will bear much fruit; apart from me you can do nothing." [18]

He is the Messiah, Mikha'el thought.

The next day, he and Elisheva had gone to the Temple to hear Yeshua teach. Then had come the awful news on the Day of Unleavened Bread: Yeshua had been crucified. At first, they didn't believe it. Later, however, Elisheva met several women in the Temple court who had witnessed the rabbi's terrible death. Mikha'el and Elisheva had returned to Korazin, saddened and dismayed.

Hoping to learn something more from one of the disciples in Capernaum, Mikha'el had walked to the nearby village. There, his friend Yochanan told him even more startling news: Yeshua had been raised from the dead. Yochanan had talked with one of the Zavdai[19] brothers, who had said, "Yeshua is alive! We have seen him!"

Mikha'el could hardly wait to get back to the insula[20] to tell Elisheva what had happened. Yeshua had risen from his tomb on the Feast of Firstfruits and had been taken back to heaven by the Almighty—just like Eliyahu.[21]

Now Mikha'el's thoughts returned to the present, and he realized, *And today, on Shavuot, Ruach HaKodesh came out of the Temple and now dwells among us, just as Yeshua promised.*

Rachel

R achel left the Temple joyfully. The promise she had heard all those years ago on the Beit-Lechem[22] hillside as she watched over her father's sheep had been true. "Today in the town of Daveed[23] a Savior has been born to you; he is Christ the LORD," the angel had proclaimed that night. "This will be a sign to you: You will find a baby wrapped in cloths and lying in a manger." [24]

---

18. John 15:1–5
19. Zebedee
20. (pl. insulae) A family household arrangement common in Capernaum and Korazin, where many rooms—residences of various family members—were built around a central courtyard.
21. Elijah
22. Bethlehem
23. David
24. Luke 2:11–12

After the heavenly vision departed, Rachel and the other shepherds had hurried into the village. With her own eyes, she had seen the baby, wrapped in soft cloths, sleeping in his mother's arms.

When Herod's soldiers slaughtered all the baby boys in Beit-Lechem, including her own little brother, Rachel thought the one the angel spoke of must have been killed, too. But Herod had not succeeded in killing him. And though the Romans had executed him, he was alive again!

That little baby in the Beit-Lechem stable had grown up to become the rabbi she had seen riding triumphantly into the city during Passover. He was Messiah, the Lamb of God!

Yochanah[25]

Yochanah fingered the huge, embossed stones of the Temple wall—Herod's stones, his great monument. But Herod had been dead for more than 25 years, and the one he had sought to kill was alive!

He's alive! Yochanah had to pinch herself to make sure she wasn't dreaming. She had to keep talking about it with the other women.

That day outside the city gates, she had felt sickened and empty, seeing his bloody body being removed from the cross. Yeshua was dead, as was all the hope she had begun to have.

Then, two days later, when she had gone to pray in the women's court at the Temple, she had heard shocking whispers: "His tomb is empty!" Three of the women who followed him had gone to his tomb at dawn that morning to take spices for his body, and they had discovered he was alive!

Yochanah smiled as she leaned her head back and raised her eyes to the royal stoa that ran the width of the southern end of the Temple platform high above, the headquarters of the Sanhedrin. Their plot had failed. They had twisted his words in their attempt to destroy him. Yet his true words had come back in power and glory.

He's alive!

---

25. Joanna

Shmu'el[26]

S hmu'el cleansed himself in the mikveh[27] at the foot of the southern stairway, then walked toward Solomon's Colonnade. Rabbi Gamaliel was to be teaching there today about the meaning of Shavuot.

Shmu'el climbed toward the Huldah Gates, fighting his way through the crowds. Making headway was difficult with the people at a standstill. Many of them seemed to be listening to someone. Shmu'el stood on tiptoe, craning his neck to see what the attraction was, and he spotted one of the disciples of the rabbi from Natzeret. What could he be saying now that his teacher had been executed?

Just a few weeks earlier, during Passover, Shmu'el himself had wanted to question the popular young rabbi about some of his teachings, particularly about what he had said regarding his yoke of Torah[28] being easy. Before Shmu'el could approach him, however, Pilate had put the man to death.

Shmu'el wondered about the truth of the rumor. It didn't make sense. Why would Pilate crucify a Jewish rabbi, no matter how controversial his teachings might be among the Temple authorities? Rome reserved that form of execution for the worst criminals and political revolutionaries.

When Shmu'el asked what others thought about the matter, he was told, "At least one of the man's talmidim was a Zealot. It's one thing to teach a different yoke; it's another to challenge the authority of the Temple as he did."

The man had probably been part of a failed plot to overthrow Rome, Shmu'el decided. That must be what had offended the authorities. *Just another false messiah,* Shmu'el thought with a sigh. Yet there had been something different about his presence . . . his words. . . .

Hadassah[29]

H adassah stood in the women's court, her hands wrapped in the ends of the shawl covering her head. Tears ran down her cheeks, as they did each time she went to the Temple. She was so overjoyed to be able to pray there again, after all her years of uncleanness—so thankful to be in the midst of God's people once more!

Today, she was listening to a rabbi teach on the words of Yirmeyahu,[30] who

---

26. Samuel
27. (pl. mikvoth) Ritual bath
28. The five books of Moses. The word *Torah* means "teachings," although it's often translated as "law."
29. Esther
30. Jeremiah

had promised that God would make a new covenant with the house of Israel. Her heart was moved as he read the words of the prophet.

> *Jahweh says, "I will put my law in their minds and write it on their hearts. I will be their God, and they will be my people. . . . They will all know me, from the least of them to the greatest," declares the Lord. "For I will forgive their wickedness and will remember their sins no more."* [31]

"Remember my sins no more, O Lord," prayed Hadassah. "As you removed my uncleanness, remove my sins."

The Galilean rabbi was gone, but Ruach HaKodesh had returned, as he had promised. She and her brother Gid'on [32] had been on the southern stairs this morning and had welcomed his presence. They had both been baptized by Yeshua's disciples in the Temple mikvoth, along with thousands of others.

Perhaps I'll not return to my father's insula in Capernaum just yet, Hadassah thought. *Perhaps I'll stay here and be part of the new community of God.*

Natan'el [33]

Natan'el welcomed the day of rest. Working at the Temple was almost impossible anyway, with all the pilgrims. Besides, this gave him time to see his father, who had come from Natzeret for the feast.

Sometimes he wished he were still working in Tiberias with his father. But Antipas needed tektons [34] here, too, to finish the stonework on the Temple. Though Herod the Great had begun rebuilding the Temple 50 years earlier, much still hadn't been completed during his reign. Judging from the building plans, Natan'el might have work here for another 40 years.

And though he missed his parents and the rest of his family, he had his wife and children with him. They lived in a comfortable little house in nearby Beit-Lechem—Daveed's town. Natan'el also enjoyed the excitement of Yerushalayim and being at the heart of things.

It's even more exciting than the theater! He chuckled, remembering his boyhood fascination with the drama at Sepphoris. That paled in comparison with the intrigue swirling around him in the streets of Yerushalayim and the Temple courts.

---

31. Jeremiah 31:31–34
32. Gideon
33. Nathanael
34. A stonemason or builder; sometimes translated as "carpenter."

The Tekton. This builder or mason (possible translations of the word *tekton* used to describe Joseph and translated as "carpenter") continues a skill that was quite familiar to those of Jesus' world. The tektons of Jesus' day worked mainly with limestone, commonly used for building. (*Eyal Bartov*)

During recent weeks, for example, Natan'el had overheard strange conversations as he knelt on the floor of the Temple Mount with his tools spread around him. Chipping away with mallet and chisel to make the decorative markings on the paving stones, he had heard the comments.

"The veil separating us from the Holy of Holies has been torn in two."

"The priests are keeping the doors shut so no one can look into the Holy of Holies, where the presence of Jahweh dwells."

Some even said the Temple veil had ripped the moment the Galilean Zealot who claimed to be the Messiah was dying on a Roman cross. Another worker later told Natan'el that it had happened at the moment the priests were making the final Passover sacrifice.

I could have told them he wasn't the Messiah, Natan'el had thought. *Everyone knows the Messiah is to come from Natzeret. He wouldn't have left Natzeret to live in Capernaum.*

El'azar[35]

Roman crosses had claimed three more patriots, among them the Galilean whose cause had held so much promise. All his revolutionary words had come to nothing.

El'azar the Zealot had just left his cousin Shi'mon[36] on the Temple steps with the other followers of the fiery young rabbi. They were claiming the man was alive—that he had died but had risen from his rocky tomb. "We're part of his kingdom now," said Shi'mon. "It's a new kingdom—different from anything we ever imagined. And we're to be his witnesses to this throughout the world!"

No! thought El'azar as he turned north on Tyropean Street toward the city gate. The Galilean's words about loving your enemies had been hard enough to believe, though a part of him had wanted to be convinced. That was especially true after the political rally during Passover, when Yeshua seemed the answer to their prayers, entering the city so triumphantly. He had marched boldly into the Temple and begun to cleanse it, just as Y'hudah[37] Maccabee had done 200 years before. Many had expected Yeshua to rally an army. Well, that certainly wasn't going to happen now. He was dead!

Aside from Shi'mon and a few others, most men in their movement felt the same way. Angered by the conspiracy of the Sanhedrin in the death of the young rabbi, however, they planned to get even. Bar-Abba,[38] who, some said, owed not only his freedom but also his life to the man, was already gathering loyalists for another plot. And at El'azar's hometown of Gamla, people were digging in and strengthening their walls. Their spies were alert for any signs of increased retaliation from Rome.

No, El'azar thought, *the Galilean's solution didn't work.*

Z'vulun[39]

Z'vulun waited for his friend Titus, who was praying in the Court of the Gentiles.[40] He smiled to himself. Titus had become a more faithful Jew than he was, and all because of his wayward son.

Z'vulun would never forget that day more than a year ago when his barge had

---

35. Eleazar
36. Simon
37. Judah
38. Barabbas; *Bar* means "son of."
39. Zebulun
40. The place where Gentiles were allowed to gather and pray by the Temple in Jerusalem. (See Temple diagram on p. 157.)

pulled into the docks at Tiberias and he had finally been able to return his friend's greetings with the words, "Yes, I've seen your son!" The young man seemed determined to stay on the other side, telling his miraculous story to anyone who would listen, so Titus had sailed across the sea with Z'vulun on his next trip.

Titus had wept at the sight of his son, looking so strong and healthy, and listened with horror and disbelief as the boy told of his descent into madness, his possession by the evil one, and his healing and restoration by the Galilean rabbi. Z'vulun and other witnesses had attested to the truth of his tale.

When Titus returned to Tiberias, he immediately set out for Capernaum, seeking the man who had saved his son from an unimaginable fate. When he found him, Titus had fallen at his feet. Since then, no one had been a more loyal follower of the teacher from Galilee.

Marcus

Tomorrow at dawn, they would return to Hippos. Marcus could hardly wait. Though not without its undercurrents, Yerushalayim was relatively quiet once more. The Jews were back again in full force for another of their strange religious celebrations, but this one didn't seem to be causing any trouble. Oh, there had been a big gathering near the southern end of the Temple today, but it had seemed peaceful enough.

"Just a lot of shouting," Gaius said after he had checked it out.

One thing Marcus wouldn't quickly forget, though, was the crucifixion a few weeks earlier. He wasn't alone. The event had made a big impression on his centurion, too. "That man should never have been crucified," he told Marcus and Gaius one night as the three shared a jug of wine and a meal. "He wasn't guilty of anything." Then he said something really strange, which made Marcus think maybe he'd had too much to drink: "I believe the man might have been the Son of God."

But Marcus couldn't explain the odd rumor that had surfaced in the barracks a few days ago. After the Galilean was dead and buried, the priests at the Temple had convinced Pilate to put a guard on the tomb. Apparently, they were afraid some of the Zealots were going to steal his body and then claim he was alive. But while the guards were on duty, an earthquake had disturbed the huge sealing stone rolled across the mouth of the tomb, and when the guards checked, the body was gone. The men swore no one had gotten past them and they hadn't fallen asleep at their post. Supposedly, the Temple priests had bribed the guards to keep their mouths shut about what had happened. But when Marcus heard who was telling the story, he wasn't surprised. It would have taken more than a bribe to keep that busybody's mouth shut.

Dead rabbis. Corrupt priests. Bloody crucifixions. Empty tombs. Missing bodies. Yes, indeed, he would be glad to get out of here. Yet Marcus couldn't shake the feeling that something significant had happened and he had been a part of it. Maybe it would all make sense when he got back to Galilee.

Asher

A great wind and tongues of fire. Our forefathers knew such things, thought Asher, *but not this generation. Truly God has poured out His Spirit on us.*[41]

When Asher had approached the city earlier this week, coming from his father's home in Azekah, he had seen the bare poles on the hill outside the gate. Though he shivered, as if their shadows cast a dark cloud, his heart rejoiced. *Pilate thinks he's dead. Herod thinks he's dead. The Sanhedrin thinks he's dead. But I know he's alive!*

Once in the city, Asher went straight to the Temple, looking for Yeshua's disciples. Somehow he knew they'd be there, and they were. And now he was among them.

After Passover, he hadn't returned to the mines at Zoar but had spent the intervening weeks with his family in the Soreq Valley so he wouldn't have so far to travel for Shavuot. He planned to return to En Gedi after the feast, hoping to find work in the king's date and palm groves.

He might even stay here in Yerushalayim for a time with the other believers, but sooner or later he knew he must leave. He didn't dread returning to the wilderness as he once might have, however, for now he had a mission. He never tired of telling people about En Gedi and the living water he had found there.

The Feast of Shavuot, also known as Pentecost or the Feast of Weeks, had been established by God through Moses. It was a day when the Jews celebrated the spring wheat harvest and what they believed was the anniversary of the day God gave Moses the Ten Commandments on Mount Sinai. To the Jews, Shavuot

---

41. Acts 2:17

commemorated both the giving of the Law and the gift of harvest.

God leaves nothing to chance. We see that over and over again in His Word. Why, then, of the seven Jewish feasts and holy days, did He send the Holy Spirit—the holy wind of God, Ruach HaKodesh—on this particular day?

First, Shavuot celebrated harvest, and Jesus had predicted there would be a great harvest. When the Holy Spirit came and rested on the disciples, who then proclaimed Jesus' message to the faithful pilgrims gathered from all over the world, the harvest Jesus had predicted throughout His ministry began. Three thousand people who were ready to become members of His new community, His new kingdom, were converted.

Leviticus 23 described Shavuot. After telling His people what they were to celebrate, when it was to be done, and who was to be involved, God made a demand. "When you harvest," He said, "don't cut the corners of your fields. Leave wheat there for the poor and the hungry, so they can provide for themselves with dignity. Thus, when you come to celebrate the harvest, when you come to give thanks for what I've given you, the true expression of your gratitude isn't your sacrifice alone. It's not the gift that you bring, and it isn't even your presence before Me. The practical proof of your thankfulness and your obedience is your concern for those in need."

Just as the Old Testament feast of Shavuot ended with concern for the poor, so the New Testament feast, which found its final fulfillment at Pentecost, ended with the believers holding all things in common and giving to each one as he or she had need. That was the practical proof to the Jews that this was truly Pentecost. It wasn't simply the conversions and the speaking in many tongues so that each could understand the message in his or her own language. It was the fact that the believers were willing to sacrifice for those in need.

As Pentecost or Shavuot Christians, we're called to supply the needs of the hungry, the lonely, the homeless, the prisoner, the sorrowing, and the broken among us. We must be willing to say, "Because I'm a Pentecost Christian, a member of the new community in which God has chosen to live—because I've experienced His presence—I care about and am willing to sacrifice for those in need."

Second, on Pentecost, the Jews of Jesus' day also remembered the time when Moses brought God's commandments down from the smoke-covered mountain. Upon reaching the bottom, Moses discovered the Israelites worshiping the calf of the abominable fertility cults of the local culture. As a result, God punished His people, and about 3,000 died that day.

God's calendar was so carefully prepared and carried out that 1,200 years after the day the Jewish people believed the Law was given and about 3,000 people died because of their rebellion against it, about 3,000 people came to life by the grace of Jesus ministered through the Spirit of God. What a vivid portrayal that the Spirit gives life and the Law condemns!

The importance of Pentecost to the Christian community can't be overemphasized. Peter's sermon very likely took place at the Temple itself. The disciples had been spending much of their time there since Jesus' death and resurrection, and they certainly would have been there to celebrate the important feast of Shavuot. Also, the sheer number of people present would require such a gathering place.

Traditionally, Christians have believed that at the moment of Jesus' death, the presence of God became accessible to all who come to Him through Jesus' sacrificial death. We're no longer separated from the presence of God. We no longer need a priest to intercede between us and our heavenly Father because our Lamb has become our Priest, the veil has been torn, and we can enter the very presence of God through our prayers. That's a powerful and wonderful concept in the Christian faith.

But when we look at the torn veil from a Jewish perspective, we can gain an even fuller understanding. As Jesus died outside the city wall, the veil that for 1,200 years had separated the people from Almighty God—represented by the Holy of Holies—was "torn in two from top to bottom" (Matthew 27:51). This was followed, within a few weeks, by Pentecost, and as Jahweh moved out of His earthly Temple in the person of His Spirit, it shook with the power and glory of His almighty presence, and immediately, tongues of fire appeared on the disciples. Fire was a symbol of the presence of God throughout the Bible. Thus, the presence of God left the stone Temple and was now dwelling in the living temple of the new Christian community. This forever changed the disciples' lives, ministry, and message.

> Don't you know that you yourselves are God's temple and that
> God's Spirit lives in you? If anyone destroys God's temple, God will
> destroy him; for God's temple is sacred, and you are that temple.
> (1 Corinthians 3:16–17)

One of the greatest blessings of Pentecost—the fulfillment of the Jewish feast of Shavuot—is that God no longer lives in a building; He lives within His people. This means that those who are committed to Him, who have believed in Jesus and have celebrated the Feast of Shavuot through His Spirit, now have the presence of God living in and through their lives.

The implications are staggering. Whereas the Old Testament believer had to go to Jerusalem to find the presence of God, we have Him right in our midst. Whereas the Old Testament believer brought his children to the Temple to show them the reality of God, we can become the reality of God's presence—His truth, love, power, and salvation—to our children and our broken world. We're proof to those around us that there is a God; we offer evidence of what He's like. What an awesome responsibility!

Perhaps God has never allowed the Temple in Jerusalem to be rebuilt because it's unnecessary now. God's presence has moved out of the building and into our hearts. We're His living stones.

> *Because he is at my right hand,*
> *I will not be shaken.*
> *Therefore my heart is glad and my tongue rejoices. . . .*
> *You have made known to me the paths of life;*
> *you will fill me with joy in your presence.*
>
> (Acts 2:25b–26,28)

Glossary

Adonai: God

Antonia: The fortress built by Herod the Great immediately north of the Temple Mount and named after his friend Mark Antony. It was used by the Roman soldiers garrisoned in Jerusalem.

Avraham: Abraham

Bar-Abba: Barabbas; *Bar* means "son of."

Bar-Talmai: Bartholomew; *Bar* means "son of."

basilikos: Means "the game of the king"; a game played with dice. One of the playing boards for this game can still be seen in Jerusalem, scratched into a huge paving stone.

Beautiful Gate: Some believe it was the eastern entrance to the women's court of the Temple, though by tradition it is the same as the Golden Gate, the eastern entrance to the Temple Mount, which today is sealed shut.

Beit-Anyah: Bethany

Beit-Lechem: Bethlehem

Beit-Pagey: Bethphage

Beth Midrash: A secondary synagogue school at which Jewish boys who had celebrated their bar mitzvahs (at 12 or 13 years of age; the term *bar mitzvah* wasn't used in Jesus' time) could study Torah and the oral traditions of their faith.

Chanoch: Enoch

Court of the Gentiles: The place where Gentiles were allowed to gather and pray by the Temple in Jerusalem.

Dani'el: Daniel

Daveed: David

Decapolis: Sometimes called "the other side"; the area on the eastern side of the Sea of Galilee and the Jordan River that included a confederation of self-ruled Hellenistic cities.

Efrayim: Ephraim

El'azar: Eleazar

Elisheva: Elizabeth

Esav: Esau

Gamla: A city on the northeastern heights (today called the Golan Heights) above the Sea of Galilee. A Zealot stronghold, it was destroyed by the Romans in A.D. 67.

Gennesaret: The Sea of Galilee; also known as the Sea of Tiberias after Herod Antipas's capital city, Tiberias, which he named for his friend the Roman emperor Tiberius.

gethsemane: An oil press; from the Hebrew *gat-shemanim*, which means "press of oils."

Gid'on: Gideon

Hadassah: Esther

Hallel: A selection comprising Psalms 113–118 and 135–136 chanted during Jewish feasts.

Hanukkah: Also known as the Feast of Dedication, which commemorated the Maccabean victory over the pagan Greeks in 167 B.C.

Haphtarah: The books of the Prophets

Har-Megiddo: Means "mound" or "tel" of Meggido; also known as Armageddon.

Herodion: Herod the Great's palace-fortress south of Jerusalem, near Bethlehem.

Hevel: Abel

insula (pl. insulae): A family household arrangement common in Capernaum and Korazin, where many rooms—residences for various family members—were built around a central courtyard.

Jahweh: God

Kefa: Peter

Kidron Valley: The valley that runs north to south along the eastern edge of Jerusalem, between the city and the Mount of Olives.

lulav: A cluster of palm, myrtle, and willow branches tied together and waved during the Feast of Sukkot.

Masada: A fortress built on a high mountain plateau on the southwestern edge of the Dead Sea. Herod the Great had an elaborate palace there.

masada: Fortress

menorah: A seven-branched candlestick

mezuzah: A hollowed-out tree branch mounted on the doorpost of a house to hold tiny, rolled parchments of Scripture. Today they're more elaborately designed and fashioned from ceramic, brass, or wood.

Mikha'el: Michael

mikveh (pl. mikvoth): Ritual bath

Moshe: Moses

Nachum: Nahum

Natan'el: Nathanael

Natzeret: Nazareth

Natzrati (pl. Natzratim): Nazarene

Ruach HaKodesh: The holy wind of God; the Holy Spirit

Salt Sea: The Dead Sea

Sea of Tiberias: The Sea of Galilee; also known as Gennesaret.

Shabbat: The Sabbath. It began at sundown on Friday night and ended at sundown on Saturday night.

Shavuot: Means "weeks"; also known as Pentecost or the Feast of Weeks. It's celebrated 50 days after the Sabbath following Passover.

Sheep Gate: Probably refers to the Tadi Gate, the gate to the north of the Temple, through which the sacrificial animals were led after being washed. This gate no longer exists.

shekel: A coin used to pay the Temple tax.

Shephelah: The foothills between the coastal plain on the Mediterranean and the Judean Mountains.

Shim'on: Simon

Shimshon: Samson

Sh'khinah: The glorious divine presence

Sh'ma: The opening prayer to all synagogue worship; it was also a statement of creed.

Shmu'el: Samuel

shofar: A ram's horn trumpet used to announce the beginning of significant times and events at the Temple in Jerusalem and in local synagogues.

s'mikhah: Ordination or authority giving one the right to make legal judgments and new interpretations of the Law and the Prophets. It could be granted by a group of elders, at least one of whom had s'mikhah himself.

Sukkot: Also known as the Feast of Tabernacles or Booths. It took place in late fall.

sukkot (sing. sukkah): Booths made of olive, palm, and myrtle branches.

talmid (pl. talmidim): A disciple or student of a rabbi whose desire was not only to know what his teacher knew but also to become like him.

Tavita: Tabitha

tekton: A stonemason or builder; sometimes translated as "carpenter."

Tiberias: The city and the sea

Torah: The five books of Moses. The word *Torah* means "teachings," although it's often translated as "law."

Towers Gate: The Damascus Gate; the northern gate of Jerusalem.

tzitzit (pl. tzitziyot): Tassel, as on a prayer shawl

Via Maris: Means "the Way of the Sea" and refers to all or part of the main trade route from Mesopotamia to Egypt that ran through Israel.

Ya'akov: Jacob or James

Yericho: Jericho

Yerushalayim: Jerusalem

Yesha'yahu: Isaiah

Yeshua: Jesus

yeshu'ah: Salvation

Y'hoshua: Joshua

Y'hudah: Judah or Judas

Yirmeyahu: Jeremiah

Yitzchak: Isaac

Yochanah: Joanna

Yochanan: John or Jonathan

Yosef: Joseph

Yoshiyahu: Josiah

Yosi: Nickname for Joseph

Zakkai: Zacchaeus

Zavdai: Zebedee

Z'karyah: Zechariah

Z'vulun: Zebulun

Annotated Bibliography

Through the years, a number of scholarly books and publications have influenced my thinking.

Richard A. Batey's *Jesus and the Forgotten City* (Grand Rapids: Baker Book House, 1991), which deals with Jesus in the context of the Hellenistic world, set me thinking about the possible connection between Jesus and the city of Sepphoris and other cities in the Decapolis, and particularly the Hellenistic theater so common to those cities.

David Biven and his organization the Jerusalem School for the Study of the Synoptic Gospels and its publication *The Jerusalem Perspective* have been and continue to be a great help to Christians who seek to understand the Jewish background of their faith.

David Flusser, from the Hebrew University in Jerusalem, in his *Judaism and the Origins of Christianity* (Jerusalem: Magnes Press, 1988), provides a significant scholarly basis for understanding the relationship between Christianity and Judaism.

Nogah Hareuveni's *Nature in Our Biblical Heritage* (Kiryat Ono, Israel: Neot Kedumim, 1980), *Tree and Shrub in Our Biblical Heritage* (1989), and *Desert and Shepherd in Our Biblical Heritage* (1991) give splendid insights into the natural setting of the Bible.

Bargil Pixner's *With Jesus Through Galilee According to the Fifth Gospel* (Rosh Pina, Israel: Corazim Publishing, 1992) provides significant background in understanding the Zealots and the Decapolis.

David H. Stern's *Jewish New Testament Commentary* (Clarksville, Md.: Jewish New Testament Publications, 1992) offers invaluable insights on individual events and passages in Jesus' life and ministry.

The workings of the olive press, described in Chapter 13, are a combination of my own research into olive presses discovered at Capernaum and descriptions of olive presses in Joan E. Taylor, "The Garden of Gethsemane," *Biblical Archaeology Review* (July/Aug. 1995): 26–35.

Marvin R. Wilson's wonderful book *Our Father Abraham: The Jewish Roots of the Christian Faith* (Grand Rapids: Eerdmans Publishing, 1989) has helped me to understand what it means to think and act Hebraically.

Brad H. Young's *Jesus the Jewish Theologian* (Peabody, Mass.: Hendrickson Publishers, 1995) and *Jesus and His Jewish Parables* (Mahwah, N.J.: Paulist Press, 1989) are good resources for better understanding that Jesus taught theology in a thoroughly Jewish manner.

First-Century Israel

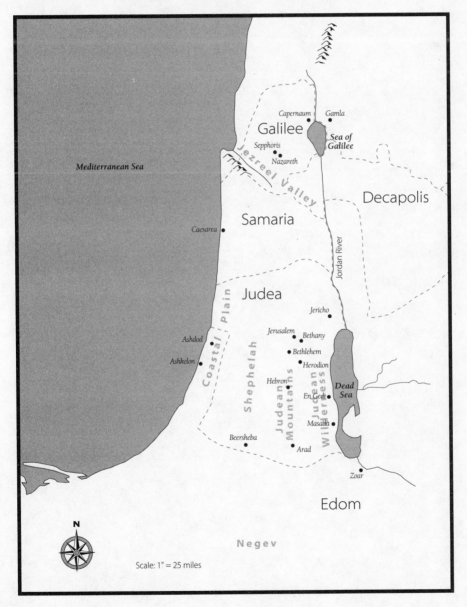

First-Century Galilee

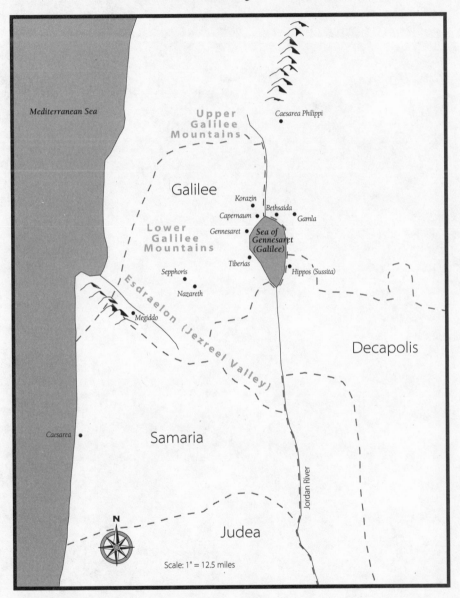

Mediterranean Sea

Upper Galilee Mountains

Caesarea Philippi

Galilee

Korazin

Bethsaida

Capernaum

Gamla

Lower Galilee Mountains

Gennesaret

Sea of Gennesaret (Galilee)

Tiberias

Hippos (Sussita)

Sepphoris

Nazareth

Esdraelon (Jezreel Valley)

Megiddo

Decapolis

Caesarea

Samaria

Jordan River

N

Judea

Scale: 1" = 12.5 miles

Transform your life through a journey of discovery into the world of the Bible

fAITH LESSONS VIDEO SERIES
Ray Vander Laan

Filmed on location in Israel, **Faith Lessons** is a unique video series that brings God's Word to life with astounding relevance. By weaving together the Bible's fascinating historical, cultural, religious, and geographical contexts, teacher and historian Ray Vander Laan reveals keen insights into the Scriptures' significance for modern believers. These illuminating "faith lessons" afford a new understanding of the Bible that will ground your convictions and transform your life.

The **Faith Lessons** video series is ideal for use at home, especially in personal and family Bible studies. Individual believers and families will gain vital insights from long ago times and cultures through this innovative approach to Bible study.

> *"Nothing has opened and illuminated the Scriptures for me quite like the Faith Lessons series."*
>
> —Dr. James Dobson

Faith Lessons on the Promised Land
Crossroads of the World
Volume One
0-310-67864-1

Faith Lessons on the Prophets & Kings of Israel
Volume Two
0-310-67865-X

Faith Lessons on the Life & Ministry of the Messiah
Volume Three
0-310-67866-8

Faith Lessons on the Death & Resurrection of the Messiah
Volume Four
0-310-67867-6

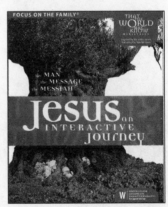

We want to hear from you. Please send your comments about this book to us in
care of the address below. Thank you.

ZondervanPublishingHouse
Grand Rapids, Michigan 49530
http://www.zondervan.com